S0-DTR-172

Japan's Dynamic Efficiency in the Global Market

Japan's Dynamic Efficiency in the Global Market

TRADE, INVESTMENT, AND ECONOMIC GROWTH

Charlie G. Turner

Foreword by
DALE W. JORGENSON

Q

Quorum Books
New York • Westport, Connecticut • London

Library of Congress Cataloging-in-Publication Data

Turner, Charlie G.
Japan's dynamic efficiency in the global market : trade, investment, and economic growth / Charlie G. Turner ; foreword by Dale W. Jorgenson.
p. cm.
Includes bibliographical references and index.
ISBN 0-89930-556-3 (alk. paper)
1. Japan—Commerce. 2. Investments, Japanese. 3. Investments, Foreign—Japan. 4. Japan—Economic conditions—1989- I. Title.
HF3824.T87 1991
337.52—dc20 90-26210

British Library Cataloguing in Publication Data is available.

Library of Congress Catalog Card Number: 90-26210
ISBN: 0-89930-556-3

First published in 1991

Quorum Books, 88 Post Road West, Westport, CT 06881
An imprint of Greenwood Publishing Group, Inc.

Printed in the United States of America

The paper used in this book complies with the Permanent Paper Standard issued by the National Information Standards Organization (Z39.48-1984).

10 9 8 7 6 5 4 3 2 1

CONTENTS

TABLES

FOREWORD

The rise of the Japanese economy has been one of the key developments of the last half of the twentieth century. In 1955, three years after the end of the American occupation that followed World War II, Japanese output per worker was one-tenth of the U.S. level. By 1985, Japanese output per worker had risen to 65 percent of that of the United States. Over these three critical decades, Japan has emerged from the ranks of developing countries to become a leading member of the community of industrialized nations.

The swiftness of the ascent of Japan from war-caused devastation has clearly taken Americans by surprise. In this book Charlie Turner turns away from adulation of the Japanese model and hysteria about Japanese competition. He presents the reader with "the truth and nothing but the truth" from the point of view of a very knowledgeable international economist. The picture that emerges is one that all of us will have to understand as we adapt our parochial viewpoints to the new realities of a global economy.

Turner first answers the question, how did Japan do it? The answer is so prosaic as to inspire disbelief: BY HARD WORK AND THRIFT. The miracle of Japanese economic development is that there was no miracle. Year after year, decade after decade, through oil crisis and political upheaval around the world, the Japanese worked hard, saved an enormous share of their growing income, and found profitable investments—first inside Japan and then in the United States and the developing world. They became leading manufacturers, skillful financiers, and astute macroeconomic policy managers.

Second, Japan has met the challenge of competing on a global scale more than any other country. However, the United States has been Japan's most important partner in the development of a global economy. Both the United States and Japan have benefited enormously from the closer integration of their economies. However, the long list of beneficiaries of rapid Japanese economic growth also includes the developing countries who have learned how to export to both Japan and the United States.

The problematical side of the Japanese success story begins in 1980 with the election of Ronald Reagan to the presidency of the United States. Reagan immediately initiated a disastrous change in U.S. economic policy, combining a massive defense buildup and a huge tax cut. These policy errors have persisted for the past decade and have undermined the position of the United States in the global economy. U.S. policy now threatens the stability of a world economic order that was largely created by American statesmen earlier in the postwar period.

Turner lays out the devastating consequences of the Reagan deficits for the world economy. He shows how the American government, misunderstanding the effects of its own radical change in policy, has lead the United States to become the world's largest debtor. The voracious appetite of the American economy for investment capital has been increasingly satisfied by foreign savers, including the Japanese. The developing world, which grew rapidly in the environment of the 1960s and 1970s, has had to subsist on a starvation diet of investment capital in the 1980s.

Charlie Turner has presented the facts about Japan and its crucial relationship to the United States and the global economy in a language that is readily understandable. Turner's story is too important to be addressed to an audience that is limited to professional economists. It concerns all of us—as citizens of the United States, as business people and employees, as borrowers and investors in the world economy. People who are hoping to reinforce their prejudices will have to look elsewhere. This is "the way it is" in Japan and the global economy in the 1990s.

Dale W. Jorgenson

ACKNOWLEDGMENTS

Competition generally assures efficiency in the allocation of resources to the productive processes of society. However, a system that leaves individuals or countries producing far below their potential, when they have not chosen such circumstances, is clearly not efficient. When asked about this issue in a public finance class at George Mason University, my professor, Ed Mayberry, said that I was interested in "dynamic efficiency." I have continued to be interested in dynamic efficiency ever since.

When I was a Ph.D. student at Harvard University, I sometimes pestered my international trade professor, Rachel McCulloch, about dynamic aspects of trade theory. Most of the theory we were learning presumed a static world with given technology and resources. She was patient with my comments in class and encouraged my further exploration of the issues. I did my dissertation on U.S. and Japanese quantitative restrictions on international trade. I was supported in my work by a National Science Foundation grant awarded to Dale Jorgenson. I worked with a Japanese economist, Masahiro Kuroda. My first detailed knowledge of Japan's economy came from this work. This book could be viewed as providing the dynamic setting for my previous work on trade barriers.

I would like to thank Wayne Talley for his support and encouragement. On his recommendation, Old Dominion University granted me research leave in the fall of 1989 when my work on this book was getting under way. My thanks also to Kehar Sangha for teaching my international economics classes while I was on leave. I would also like to thank my students at Old Dominion, the University of Oklahoma, and Harvard for teaching me how to explain economic theory clearly. I am sure that any of them reading this book will be surprised that I have said what I have to say without the graphs that are a constant part of my classroom presentation.

I also want to thank my family. My brother, Joseph Turner, was attached to the U.S. embassy in Tokyo for four years. While he was sometimes skeptical of my writing about Japan when I had never been there, he had a continuing interest in the work I was doing. My son, David, who is living in London, encouraged me not to be too parochial and to include Europe in my analysis. Last and most importantly, I want to thank my wife, Elizabeth Monk-Turner. She read through the manuscript and gave me detailed comments. The result is a book that should be understandable to intelligent readers of all disciplines rather than being available only to other economists.

1 Japan and the Dynamic Global Economy

There is widespread recognition that Japan is a major force in the global economy as we enter the last decade of the twentieth century. Reading the financial press reveals that Japan is the world's largest creditor nation. Japan has large trade surpluses, especially with the United States. Japan imposes quotas on imports of rice, beef, and other commodities, and has an intricate distribution network that makes it hard for U.S. firms to sell there. The Japanese failure to buy U.S. Treasury bonds during an auction would send U.S. interest rates soaring. Japanese firms are buying U.S. firms and real estate.

The interconnections among Japan's effects on trade flows, international capital markets, and macroeconomic performances are not widely understood. This book examines Japan's role in the dynamic global economy in a dispassionate, analytical way. I am an international economist, and the approach I use in this undertaking is to apply economic analysis to the Japanese economy. International economics has developed rigorous theoretical models to explain why countries trade with each other and the consequences of such trade. Issues of trade balance, commercial policy, international capital flows, and economic growth have all been addressed at great length in theoretical and empirical ways by international economists.

The approach taken in this book is to ask what information is necessary to understand how any national economy fits into the dynamic global economy, and then to gather such information for Japan. By taking what amounts to an universalist approach and filling in the details on

Japan, I hope that this study will provide new insight to those interested in understanding Japan. It seems to me that too many authors are either Japanophiles or Japanophobes. While my study exhibits the intellectual biases of an international economist, I believe it to be objective as far as Japan is concerned. This book is intended to give the reader an understanding of how Japan's economy functions within the dynamic global economy. Major issues of importance in understanding how the global economy functions are examined, while presenting particular information about Japan. The impact of Japanese developments in production, technology, trade policy, and finance on the United States and the rest of the global economy is examined, as is the impact on Japan of global developments in these areas.

Corporations and countries function within a dynamic global economy. When corporations decide to invest in plant and equipment, they need to form expectations about the conditions of global production over the life of the proposed plant. It is not safe to ignore the activities of corporations in other countries. Nor should corporations restrict their analyses to supply and demand conditions anticipated for the next year or two. Corporate strategy and planning must be concerned with all major global participants over a relatively long period of time.

Individuals also need to be aware of the dynamic global economy. Most people will gain their lifetime earnings from wages and salaries. The decision regarding which career or vocation to follow is one that ideally would incorporate information about likely global developments over the next forty years. Further, individuals need to actively determine what investments to undertake to provide for their retirement. If an individual's principal retirement vehicle is a company pension, an appreciation of global events can still be important as LTV steel workers learned when their company went bankrupt. An understanding of the global economy can result in better judgments. A diversified international portfolio can provide higher expected returns with less risk than one that is limited to one national economy (Solnick, 1988).

Fortunately, relative returns within the labor market are reasonably stable. The information available to people entering the labor force at one point in time is useful as a prediction of relative earnings twenty years hence. Potential workers can decide how much education and training to obtain before entering the labor force. The major exception is in regard to work in industries with some monopolistic power. The extra wages earned by such workers can be wiped out if the industries themselves lose their monopoly power. Steel workers found this out the hard way in the mid-1980s.

Japan is a major participant in today's dynamic global economy. Japan has the second-largest market-oriented economy in the world. It continues to have the highest growth rate, the highest savings rate, and the highest level of productivity increases in the industrial world. Its education of engineers and scientists, and consequent product innovations, continue apace. These and other attributes cause Japan to be a major source of change in the dynamic global economy. Thus, any firm concerned with functioning in the global economy should study Japan to better understand likely changes in the global economy.

Patterns of international trade and investment can only be fully appreciated when intertemporal aspects of optimization are considered. Decisions regarding production and distribution over a long time period are based on judgments about product prices, exchange rates, trade barriers, technological change, available resources, global demand, and other issues. These judgments must be made either explicitly or implicitly. Making an informed, explicit judgment is likely to be better than acting on vaguely formed ideas. This book provides a guide to understanding Japanese trade and investment as important parts of the dynamic global economy.

THE BENEFITS OF TRADE

A country enters into international commerce and remains open to trade because it is in its self-interest to do so. International trade theory explains how various groups in the economy are affected by trade. When a country moves from no trade to free trade, everyone in the society *could* be made better off. In general, some groups in the society would be worse off, but if an appropriate system of taxes and transfers were put into place, the losers could be compensated and there would still be winners remaining (Dixit and Norman, 1980). How do these benefits from trade come about? Who is helped and who is hurt?

Every country in the world has some level of international trade. Further, every country restricts trade to some extent. The discussion of going from no trade to free trade is a hypothetical one. By examining the changes that occur from such a switch, we can gain insights as to what happens when a country moves from very restricted trade to relatively free trade. This is the kind of transition that Mexico is currently experiencing.

Benefits from international trade are measured, as in most of economic analysis, by consumer welfare. Much popular criticism of international trade is directed toward other issues such as trade imbalances, lost jobs, or market losses. Is consumer welfare the appropriate measure? I believe it is. Of course, I am an economist, so I may be biased, but let me explain why economists use consumer welfare.

Everyone is a consumer. Our total lifetime consumption is limited by our lifetime earnings and net transfers from others including the government, such as inheritances or welfare. Generally, we do not have as many consumption goods as we would like. We would be happier—have higher welfare—if we had more consumption. Therefore, any change that would allow us to consume more of everything would mean a positive increase in our welfare.

Sometimes the argument is made that jobs are the most important target for economic policy. However, there are usually implicit assumptions behind such a statement. Most often, people assume that the jobs obtained will pay the prevailing wage, or perhaps even more. A further assumption is that prices of goods will stay about the same. With these assumptions, the promotion of additional jobs translates into higher real income, which means that, as consumers, we will have higher welfare. In other words, promoting employment at current wages and prices is consistent with the goal of maximizing consumer welfare. This is why virtually all economists believe an economic system that promotes full employment is better than one that substantially underutilizes its human resources.

On the other hand, providing jobs at wages substantially lower than the prevailing wage would not be a great accomplishment. If General Motors proposed to offer jobs at $1 per day in exchange for a permanent ban on automobile imports, the government should reject the proposal. General Motors would get the better of the deal. It would gain billions of dollars by selling more cars at higher prices, and no one would want the jobs offered. Of course, General Motors would have to pay more than $1 a day to the workers producing its cars.

When economists talk about consumer welfare, we include in our calculations earnings from work and the use of other resources that people own. Factors of production are the inputs to the production process. The most important factor of production is labor. The next most important is capital, by which economists mean machines, plant, and other equipment. The total of such production factors that we as a society possess, together with known technology, determines what we can produce. In a closed economy, the output of the economy is distributed solely to the members of the society. In a perfectly competitive economy, the total product is distributed through a market system to those willing to pay for the commodities. People's ability to pay depends on their income. Their income depends on how much of the factors of production they own, and on the prices paid for those factors of production.

In a closed economy, we can theoretically calculate the level of welfare in the society by looking at what we can consume. Assuming our incomes and prices remain constant, we know the amount of various goods that we can afford. As indicated, what we can consume depends on the factors of production available, technology, and how efficiently our economic system allocates resources to production processes.

When a closed economy is thrown open to trade, we can see how changes are effected in the economy. First, imagine what would happen if there were no change in production of goods in the economy. In this case, if relative prices of foreign goods were the same as our relative prices in the closed economy, there would be no incentive to trade and nothing would change. If the prices of some goods relative to other goods differed in the domestic and foreign economies, there would be an incentive to exchange goods. We would export those goods that are relatively cheaper in our economy and import those goods that are relatively more expensive in our economy. As a consequence, the price of the relatively cheap goods would rise in our economy and the price of the relatively expensive goods would fall. The foreign countries would undergo a similar process, but their relatively cheap goods would be those that we import because they are relatively expensive here.

In this scenario, where no change in production occurs, there are still winners and losers. Consumers of the goods whose prices fall benefit from trade, while those owning or producing such goods when trade occurs lose. Likewise, consumers of goods whose relative prices rise are made worse off. An individual's welfare change is uncertain in such a case; he or she could be better off or worse off. How, then, do we know that society as a whole could be better off? Remember, we are exchanging goods that are relatively cheap for goods that are relatively dear in our pretrade society. We are thus able to consume at free trade prices a mixture of commodities that was impossible for us to produce. Further, at original pretrade prices the bundle we now consume was worth more than our total national output. When China gave up the idea of self-sufficiency and increased trade with the West, it was able to increase its consumption of TVs and cars without reducing consumption of textiles (which it exports) by as large a value amount. If the winners in the process gave up just enough in taxes to keep the losers even with their pretrade position, there would still be gains left over.

When production is allowed to change, the situation becomes more complicated, but the end result is the same. When prices change due to international trade, producers in a competitive economy shift production toward the commodity whose price rose. This shift in production causes the prices of the factors of production that are used intensively in producing such commodities to rise relative to other factor prices. Further, it can be shown, as Wolfgang Stolper and Paul Samuelson (1941) did, that the factor price changes more, on a percentage basis, than the commodity does. The result is that the real income of some factor owners will increase and the real income of other factor owners will decrease. Not surprisingly, the opponents of free trade are almost always found among the factor owners who lose in this process. The reason for their opposition is that, even though a redistribution from winners to losers is possible, it is seldom undertaken.

The change in production results in the country producing more goods that are more valuable at the new prices (with trade) than the goods that were previously produced. In short, the country as a whole is even better off than when production was not allowed to change. Of course, changing production also entails shifting workers from one industry to another. There could be some frictional unemployment during the transition.

If international trade permits the consumption of goods that previously were unavailable, then the benefits are even greater than those indicated above. Such items can range from tropical fruits to inventions not available in the domestic economy. The Japanese invention of the bread machine that bakes individual loaves of bread in four hours or overnight is just one example.

THE BENEFITS FROM GLOBAL INVESTMENT

Just as free trade has the potential to benefit each country on balance, so too do free investment flows. The gains accrue to lenders in the surplus country and to borrowers in the deficit country. For net investment to occur, the lending country must run a surplus on current account with the rest of the world. Likewise, the borrowing country must run a deficit.

Everything else the same, a lending country will have a higher real interest rate and return on capital because of the lending. The losers in the lending country are those who want to borrow on net, that is, who owe more than they lend. However, by definition, at the going interest rate, more money is loaned than borrowed if the country has a net outflow of financial capital. Thus, if the lenders compensated the borrowers, there would be some gain left over. In the borrowing country, the real interest rate and the return on capital would be lower due to international borrowing, all else the same. The borrowers could compensate the losers (domestic lenders) and still have something left over. The country would have a net benefit.

The benefits mentioned in this analysis presume perfect markets and borrowing and lending for private purposes. Financial capital flows to finance government deficits will still tend to have the indicated effects on real interest rates, but the overall welfare effects will depend on whether government policies are appropriate. Wasteful or misguided policies have harmful consequences. If international lending permits such policies to continue for long or at a high level, then such lending could have adverse consequences. Purportedly, this is what happened in some of the Latin American countries during the 1970s. However, real income per capita did increase in the Latin American debtor countries like Brazil and Mexico. It is clear these countries overborrowed, given the global economic slowdown and high interest rates in the early 1980s. It is not clear how much of the money borrowed was actually "wasted." The mere existence of bad government policies that result in international borrowing is not sufficient to prove international lending harmful.

A COMPARATIVE VIEW OF JAPAN IN THE DYNAMIC GLOBAL ECONOMY

We can best understand Japan's functioning within the dynamic global economy by comparing Japan with other countries at various points in time. I have chosen to examine the United States, West Germany, and Mexico, in addition to Japan. The United States was chosen because it has been the dominant economic power in the post–World War II period and because it happens to be my country. West Germany was chosen since it is a major economic force in the European Economic Community (EEC). Mexico was selected as a developing country of special importance to the United States. By comparing developments within these countries, we can gain insight into the economic forces in the dynamic global economy.

Table 1.1 reports information on population, gross national product (GNP), and the factors of production in each of the four countries at five different points in time. The time points are 1955, 1965, 1975, 1985, and estimates for 1995. We can see how the comparative status of the countries has changed through time. It is basically a dynamic comparative analysis.

International trade theory indicates that a country will have a comparative advantage in the commodities that the country produces at relatively lower cost than other countries. In general, a country will have a lower cost in production of those commodities which use inputs that are abundant in that country. Abundance and use of inputs are measured on a relative basis. Thus, by looking at the relative abundance of professional and technical personnel in 1965, we can see that the United States has 115 per 1,000 workers, which is higher than any other country. The United States is then expected to export, in 1965, goods that use relatively high levels of professional and technical personnel. Similarly, Japan, in 1985, has more capital per worker than other countries and can be expected to export goods that use capital intensively. Japanese relative abundance of capital is expected to be even greater by 1995. Chapters 2 and 3 build on this information to explain Japanese export and import patterns.

The information presented in Table 1.1 also provides insights into the economic growth of Japan and the other listed countries. The productivity of workers is generally a function of their skill and training, the capital available for their use, and land and other resources used in production. A country's gross national product is simply the output per worker times the number of workers in the society. By providing the demographic information on population per worker, we could easily construct per capita GNP.

A comparison of exports relative to GNP is provided as a measure of the dependence of a country on foreign trade. By tracking this measure

Table 1.1
Comparative Data on Output and Factors of Production over Time, Japan, United States, West Germany, and Mexico

	1955	1965	1975	1985	1995[a]
Japan					
Active work force (millions)	40	49	54	60	63
People per worker	2.2	2.0	2.1	2.0	2.0
GNP per worker (1988 dollars)	$ 2,584	$ 6,514	$18,850	$24,345	$61,863
Other factors per 1,000 workers					
Professional and technical	NA	51	78	90	140
Land (square miles)	3.7	2.9	2.6	2.4	2.3
Capital (millions of 1988 dollars)	$2.7	$10.3	$40.3	$47.2	$109.3
Ratio of exports to GNP	.13	.11	.14	.16	.14
United States					
Active work force (millions)	71	78	95	117	129
People per worker	2.4	2.5	2.2	2.0	2.0
GNP per worker (1988 dollars)	$25,449	$31,514	$32,994	$37,433	$45,245
Other factors per 1,000 workers					
Professional and technical	NA	115	139	148	153
Land (square miles)	51.1	46.1	38.1	30.8	28.0
Capital (millions of 1988 dollars)	$21.7	$30.6	$39.7	$35.7	$49.5
Ratio of exports to GNP	.04	.05	.08	.07	.13
West Germany					
Active work force (millions)	25	27	27	29	29
People per worker	2.0	2.1	2.3	2.1	2.1
GNP per worker (1988 dollars)	$ 7,545	$15,381	$31,817	$23,823	$44,881
Other factors per 1,000 workers					
Professional and technical	NA	76	128	139	140
Land (square miles)	3.8	3.6	3.6	3.3	3.3
Capital (millions of 1988 dollars)	$ 6.9	$19.0	$41.2	$42.2	$68.7
Ratio of exports to GNP	.20	.19	.26	.35	.42
Mexico					
Active work force (millions)	10	11	17	22	34
People per worker	3.1	3.1	3.6	3.0	2.9
GNP per worker (1988 dollars)	$ 3,287	$ 6,315	$ 7,969	$ 5,228	$9,962
Other factors per 1,000 workers					
Professional and technical	NA	36	62	66	73
Land (square miles)	79.3	67.2	45.9	34.5	22.2
Capital (millions of 1988 dollars)	$ 1.9	$ 3.3	$ 9.7	$10.8	$12.1
Ratio of exports to GNP	.15	.10	.07	.19	.20

Sources: International Labour Office, various years; International Monetary Fund, *International Financial Statistics,* various years; OECD (1989); *Times Atlas;* United Nations, *Yearbook of National Accounts Statistics* and *World Population Prospects,* various years; United States, *Business Conditions Digest* and *Economic Report of the President,* various years.

[a] Estimated.

over time, we can see the degree of increasing interdependence among economies. Also, by comparing across countries, we can see relative dependence on international trade.

The active workforce ranges from 10 million in Mexico in 1955 to 129 million in the United States in 1995. The increase in the active workforce from 1955 to 1995 is lowest for West Germany (16%) and highest for Mexico (240%). Japan's increase in the work force over this period is 57 percent, and the United States had an increase of 82 percent.

The number of people per worker ranges from 2.0 to 3.6. This is simply the ratio of the total population to the number of active workers in a country. A ratio of 2.0 indicates that the average worker in the country is supporting two people, himself or herself and one dependent. Mexico has 2.9–3.6 people per worker, compared to the more industrialized countries with 2.0–2.5 people per worker. This undoubtedly reflects Mexico's faster population growth, greater agrarian sector, and perhaps more of a non-reported unofficial sector.

GNP per worker is reported in 1988 dollars. The dollar amounts are translated at market exchange rates, and so may overstate or understate differences with the United States depending on fluctuations in real purchasing power in different currencies. Kravis et al. (1975) have dealt with this problem at length, but I have used the simpler exchange rate translation. One effect is to exaggerate the relative GNP and capital stock of the United States in 1985 when the dollar was overvalued.

GNP per worker declined in Germany in dollar terms from 1975, even though German real income in deutsche marks did not decline. Projected dollar increases in GNP from 1985 to 1995 are especially sharp for the nondollar countries because the dollar has declined in real terms since 1985. I have assumed that the 1988 real exchange rates will hold for the rest of the period.

Japanese GNP per worker, which is already greater than U.S. GNP per worker (at current exchange rates), will rise to be 37 percent more than the U.S. level by 1995 if current trends continue. This is an amazing development, given that Japan's GNP per worker was only 10 percent of the U.S. level in 1955. Germany will have a GNP per worker of $44,881, or 99 percent of the U.S. level, in 1995. This is an increase from 30 percent of the U.S. level in 1955 and 49 percent of the U.S. level in 1965, but it is not much of a change from the 96 percent of the U.S. level that Germany had in 1975. Mexico is projected to have a GNP per worker of $9,962 in 1995. This is based on relatively optimistic assumptions about restoring the Mexican economy to an efficient level of operation. Even so, Mexico's relative GNP per worker was highest in 1975 when it was 24 percent of the U.S. level. The fall in the price of oil, Mexico's major export, and the debt crisis have taken their toll on Mexican economic growth.

Why does a country's GNP per worker grow? Denison (1967) identifies the amount and quality of education, capital per worker, and technological change as important elements contributing to economic growth. Technology is, to a degree, shared by all participants in the global economy. Improvements in technology over time should raise output per worker in all countries if the other factors of production per worker stay the same. Leamer (1984) developed a model of world production and trade based on endowments of detailed factors of production. He identified three types of labor and four types of land, for example.

Table 1.1, shows the level of four factors of production. In addition to workers, the other three factors are highly skilled workers (professional and technical personnel), land, and capital. These three factors are presented in terms of factors per 1,000 workers. When possible, these factors are given for 1955, 1965, 1975, 1985, and estimated for 1995.

The most direct cause of the changes in GNP per worker is the amount of capital per worker. As machinery or other kinds of capital per worker increases, the average worker will be able to produce more with each hour of labor. In the United States, capital per 1,000 workers went from $21.7 million in 1955 to $49.5 million in 1995, an increase of 128 percent. These figures are in 1988 dollars, so the change represents a real increase in plant and equipment per worker. GNP per worker increased 78 percent over this same period. Capital per worker decreased in the United States between 1975 and 1985; in 1985, it was only 90 percent of its level in 1975.

In Japan, capital per 1,000 workers went from $2.7 million in 1955 to $109.3 million 1988 dollars in 1995. This is an increase of 3,948 percent. GNP per worker went up 2,294 percent during the same period. It appears that the tremendous increase in capital per worker in Japan, which was made possible by Japan's high savings rate and investment level, led to a tremendous increase in GNP per worker. The United States had a much lower relative increase in capital per worker and a much lower increase in GNP per worker.

Land per worker does not appear to have a major effect on GNP per worker. This is not surprising in light of the relatively small role of agriculture in the modern economy. In Japan, land per 1,000 workers declined from 3.7 square miles in 1955 to 2.3 square miles in 1995. This is a 28 percent decline. Mexico had the highest amount of land per 1,000 workers in 1955, at 79.3 square miles. Yet Mexico had the lowest per worker GNP in that year.

Professional and technical personnel per 1,000 workers ranges from 36 in Mexico in 1965 to 153 in the United States in 1995. For Japan the range has been from 51 in 1965 to 140 in 1995. This goes from 44 percent of the U.S. level in 1965 to 93 percent in 1995. Japan and West Germany have the same level of professional and technical personnel per 1,000 workers presently. Mexico's lower output per worker expected in 1995 is reflected in its lower professional and technical ratio per worker (48 percent of the U.S. level), as well as its lower capital per worker (24 percent of the U.S. level).

The last statistic reported in table 1.1 is the ratio of exports to GNP.

This provides a measure of a country's openness to or dependence on international trade. The range of this ratio is from .04 in the United States in 1955 to .42 in West Germany in 1995. West Germany has consistently had a far higher export to GNP ratio than the other three countries. This indicates that Germany is more sensitive to economic developments in its trading partners. It is, in a sense, more dependent on export markets for maintaining its level of output and employment. In 1955, Japan had an export to GNP ratio that was 65 percent of that of West Germany. The highest U.S. ratio relative to West Germany's was 31 percent in 1975. Mexico's ratio of .07 in 1975 was lower than the U.S. ratio of .08 in that year. Otherwise, the U.S. ratio has been lower than the other three countries' throughout the period. The dip in U.S. exports relative to GNP from 1975 to 1985 is largely a result of U.S. macro policies of high growth and an overvalued dollar, which caused U.S. manufacturers to be at a competitive disadvantage. There has been a general trend for the export to GNP ratio to increase over the postwar period, reflecting the rapid growth in international trade. Japan's growth in this ratio (23 percent from 1955 to 1985) is actually the smallest percentage change among the four countries. Japan's trade has grown tremendously, but its GNP and domestic market have grown nearly as fast. Japan's dependence on export markets to maintain its output has not changed much since the 1950s. This is a little surprising to citizens of Japan's trading partners, since we see a lot more Japanese goods. Basically, there are more Japanese goods consumed everywhere because more are produced.

GUIDE TO THE REST OF THIS BOOK

Japanese Trade

Japanese export and import patterns are a result of a complex interaction between Japan and the rest of the globe. Chapters 2–5 explain the pattern of Japanese trade in a realistic dynamic framework, explicitly recognizing imperfect competition. The chapters on Japanese exports and imports explain the direction of trade. Chapters 4 and 5 offer a discussion of trade barriers. The effects these barriers have had and will continue to have are presented.

Japan has developed as a global participant even though it has imposed, and faced, many trade barriers. The current pattern of Japanese trade and trade barriers are analyzed, as are historical patterns of trade and barriers to trade. Historical patterns of trade, Japan's trade barriers, and other countries' barriers against Japanese goods are shown by decade in the postwar period. Projections of the 1990s trade patterns are provided, based on present and likely levels of Japanese and global resources and demands. Included in these projections are likely policy developments regarding trade barriers. Of course, any such projections are speculative, consisting of informed judgments. However, businesses are forced to make such judgments every time they undertake a long-term capital investment. The processes and sources used by the author to arrive at such projections will be explicit and will provide a guide for the reader to make appropriate adjustments as time reveals new developments.

Macroeconomics and Investment

Trade would be balanced if residents and the government of one country could not borrow from another country. Trade surpluses or deficits could occur with shifts in holdings of precious metals or other international reserves, but these would be short run in nature. Trade deficits and surpluses have to be explained by differences in macroeconomic variables and policies. Investments in other countries by residents of Japan and investments in Japan by foreign residents are important aspects of the dynamic global economy.

Macroeconomic forces initiated in Japan have an important impact on the rest of the world, and macroeconomic forces initiated in the rest of the world impact Japan. Chapter 6 provides a guide to how Japan differs from the rest of the world in terms of its macroeconomic variables, and how these differences impact the rest of the world. For instance, the high Japanese savings rate leads to current account surpluses and an outflow of Japanese capital when Japanese economic growth and investment slow. Chapter 7 provides a guide to how developments in the macroeconomies of the rest of the world impact Japan. The U.S. trade deficit, the oil shock, and similar events have repercussions on the Japanese economy.

Japanese investment patterns in the rest of the world and foreign investment in Japan are examined in chapters 8 and 9. An equilibrium international arbitrage pricing model of investment is used as a guide to understanding investment patterns. Current patterns of investment are analyzed. Historical patterns are explored in the postwar period.

Japan, the United States, and LDCs

Japan's relationship with the United States and relationships with less developed countries (LDCs) are dealt with in chapters 10 and 11. The United States has had a special relationship with Japan throughout the postwar period. The occupation and subsequent political and military developments have had important implications for Japan's economic performance.

Japan is increasing its aid to LDCs. Japan has also developed from being an LDC within a short period of time, and thus serves as a model for LDCs. The likely impact of Japanese foreign direct investment and official aid on LDCs is presented.

Summary

An overall assessment of Japan's place in the dynamic global economy is presented in chapter 12. This chapter summarizes material presented earlier in the book. It constitutes a summary guide to Japan's current and likely future impact within the global economy.

NOTES ON TABLE 1.1

All dollar amounts were converted from current year dollars to 1988 dollars by using the GNP price deflator index reported in the *President's Economic Report* and the *Business Conditions Digest.* Fixed capital was calculated as simply 1.25 times the five-year total of fixed capital formation. This provides a result not too different from the more detailed procedure followed by Leamer (1984) which provides for an average life of equipment of fifteen years. All statistics reported in currencies other than dollars were translated at market average exchange rates for the year in which the translation was made.

Projections for 1995 were made as follows: Population came from the medium-range projections of the U.N. World Population Prospects. The economically active population was considered to be the same portion of the population as in the latest available U.N. Yearbook of Labour Statistics, except for Mexico, which was assumed to have a participation rate of 35 percent, up from 33 percent in 1985. Professional and technical workers per 1,000 workers figures were projected to increase for the whole period at the same rate at which they had increased in the 1985–87 period. The average gross fixed capital formation for 1991–95 was estimated as the 1988 level plus the change from 1982 to 1988. This average was then multiplied by five years to get the five-year total. This was then multiplied by 1.25 to get the total capital stock. The capital stock was translated to dollars at the 1988 exchange rates. This basically presumes that 1995 real exchange rates will be relatively close to those in 1988. Projections of GNP, exports, and imports for the industrialized countries converted all figures to 1988 dollars and assumed Organization for Economic Cooperation and Development (OECD) projections of real growth for 1989 and 1990 held for the remaining time to 1995. Exports were assumed to be the lesser of estimated imports or exports using these projections. For Mexico, optimistic assumptions were made regarding a slight increase in capital per worker and a real increase in GNP per worker of 25 percent over 1975. This would be an improvement of 91 percent in GNP per worker over 1985. Nevertheless, Mexican GNP per worker would remain at only 22 percent of the U.S. level.

2 JAPANESE EXPORT PATTERNS

The pattern and importance of Japanese exports have changed dramatically over the last forty years. The Japanese started the postwar period with a relatively low level of exports. Japan's exports were only 2 percent of world exports. Most of the 1955 exports of Japan (58%) were in basic industries such as textiles and steel. By 1995, Japanese exports are expected to be 10 percent of world exports, with 74 percent of them in machinery and transportation equipment.

We need to understand Japanese export patterns in the context of the dynamic global economy. Japan has experienced very rapid growth over the last forty years. Its gross national product (GNP), capital, and number of technical and professional workers have grown rapidly relative to its work force. As a consequence, its pattern of exports and imports has changed over this period.

Looking at the changes that have occurred, it is clear that forces other than just growth of such economic factors are also at work in shaping the pattern of Japanese exports. The major industries that produce most of Japan's exports are those industries that have had some of the most rapid growth in the last forty years. Industries like automobiles, computers, and consumer electronics have experienced rapid growth since the 1950s. Computers, color televisions, and video cassette recorders were not even available as commercial products forty years ago.

These industries also have some degree of oligopoly power, with consequent market positioning and strategy by firms (Porter, 1986). Oligopolistic firms will be trying to maintain and expand market share, to discourage other firms from entering the industry. This might sometimes require lower profit margins for a period of time when entry by others would otherwise be likely. If a firm develops a large presence in an industry during its early expansion, there will be a deterrence to other firms entering the industry as the industry matures. The first to enter successfully in a major way can dominate the industry. Japanese firms have been very successful at pursuing such oligopoly strategy. The fact that Japan has been undergoing a period of tremendous expansion has enabled Japanese firms to occupy positions quickly in areas of greatest growth opportunities. Japan's high savings rate has allowed tremendous manufacturing flexibility to pursue those markets that were expected to grow the fastest. Together, dynamic comparative advantage and strategic oligopoly behavior explain Japan's export patterns fairly well.

The United States and the Pacific Rim countries are important export markets for the Japanese. West Germany and other members of the European Economic Community (EEC) are smaller export markets for the Japanese than would be expected from their overall level of imports. There appears to be some diverting of European imports away from Japan. The relative level of exports to various countries also reveals the importance of the United States and the Pacific Rim countries. West Germany and other members of the EEC have restricted Japanese exports to their countries.

Japan has become a major exporter of machinery and transportation equipment. If we define export dependence of a country as the degree to which its production and growth depend on export markets, then Japan has some export dependency. All countries that are integrated into the global trading system have some industries with a high level of exports relative to domestic production. Japan is dependent on exports in this way. However, Japan is still much less dependent on export markets than West Germany is. The perception that Japan produces mostly for export simply does not match the facts.

A country gains from trade because it can achieve a level of consumption that is higher than it would be if no trade took place. This is achieved by exporting those goods that would be relatively cheap if the country's economy were closed and importing those goods that would be relatively expensive. As a consequence, the average standard of living in the country will be higher even though some groups in society may be made worse off by trade. The theoretical determination of Japan's export patterns should be a matter of determining which goods would be relatively cheap in Japan if it were a closed economy.

DYNAMIC COMPARATIVE ADVANTAGE

Prices in a market economy are set by supply and demand. If we abstract from differences in preferences for goods in various countries, then differences in prices in closed economies will reflect differences in production costs. If a country can produce a commodity less expensively relative to other goods produced by its trading partners, it is said to have a comparative advantage in producing that commodity. Since it is relative production costs that are important, each country must have a comparative advantage in producing at least one good unless relative prices are the same in all countries. We generally expect countries to export goods in which they have a comparative advantage.

The idea of comparative advantage was developed by David Ricardo (1817) during the debates on the British Corn Laws. Such advantage can occur because of differences in technology or because of differences in endowments of resources and other factors of production. It is important to remember that comparative advantage is defined in terms of the relative cost of production. If a country can make all commodities with fewer work hours and other inputs, that country has an absolute advantage in producing all commodities. Nevertheless, it is beneficial for the country to trade by exporting those goods in which it has a comparative advantage.

Lower relative production costs due to different relative endowments of the factors of production are harder to understand than differences due to technology alone. The argument is basically that countries with relatively large amounts of land would have low land rents relative to wages when producing in isolation. Consequently, they will produce goods that use land intensively at relatively low prices. Thus, when trade occurs, they will have a comparative advantage in producing land-intensive goods. These include corn, wheat, lumber, etc. They will export those goods that intensively use those factors of production that they have in relative abundance. A good, rigorous treatment of this theory, which is a generalized Heckscher-Ohlin theory, is presented by Deardorff (1982).

Unfortunately, the real world is even more complicated than the generalized Heckscher-Ohlin theory that has given many international economics students sleepless nights and headaches. The most important factors of production are labor and capital. These factors change over time. They change in quantity, and perhaps even more important, in quality. Therefore, over time, comparative advantage will change, dependent on different rates of capital accumulation, population growth, and educational changes. Further, capital takes time to put in place and then lasts for a relatively long period of time. These effects have been studied by Klein (1973), Oniki and Uzawa (1965), and others. Choosing the optimal behavior in such a changing world is no simple task. Dynamic comparative advantage should nevertheless give information on how to understand past and present trade patterns and what we can expect in the future.

While most economic models assume perfect competition, we know that monopoly power exists in various markets. Helpman and Krugman (1985) have written extensively on the effects of imperfect competition on trade theory. Economies of scale and imperfect competition are very important in a dynamic trading context. A company will consider existing firms in the market when contemplating investment in a market characterized by monopoly or oligopoly power. Hence, a firm that quickly moves into an industry and expands its plant can dissuade others from entering that industry (Spence, 1976). This will be especially true where fixed plant and development costs are large relative to variable costs. Automobiles and computers are two such industries. Economies of scale can be captured by any firm producing for the global economy, regardless of the size of its domestic market. The only requirements are that the barriers to trade be low and that they will remain low. Transportation cost as a percent of value is one such barrier. More importantly, tariffs and nontariff barriers need to be low and there must be expectations of future fair treatment.

The world trading system since World War II has been favorable for international trade. The world has gone through a number of multilateral trade negotiations that have facilitated trade and economic growth. This has greatly aided Japan's development over this period. Japan needed ready access to raw materials and to foreign markets to sell products to pay for its imports. Relative to other large economies like the United States and the Soviet Union, Japan would be harmed much more by a complete cessation of trade. In that sense, Japan is more dependent on trade and has a greater interest in development of an even freer trade environment.

JAPAN'S EXPORTS

Changes in Japan's export pattern in the dynamic global economy are shown in four tables (tables 2.1–2.4). With these, we can see how Japan's comparative advantage has changed since 1955 and how trade with certain countries has become more important to Japan. Further, the importance of Japan's trade as a source of imports to these countries has increased dramatically. Commodity categories and industries that account for the largest share of Japan's exports are examined. We see that Japan's exports as a share of its total supply are not as great as perceived.

There is a widely held perception in the United States that Japan produces most of its goods for export to the United States and other export markets. This is simply not true. As can be seen in table 2.4, in 1985, transport equipment (mostly automobiles) was the only International Standard Industrial Category (ISIC) at the three-digit level (manufacturing), that had more than a third of supply exported. (The United Nations established the ISIC to standardize data on industrial output.) This means that almost two-thirds of the automobiles built in Japan stay in Japan.

Even though Japanese exports have increased rapidly over the last forty years, this is primarily due to Japan's rapid economic growth. Export-led growth is usually characterized as a set of policies to induce growth in export industries. This growth in exports in turn causes a general growth in output through increased employment and investment. Growth in the Japanese economy has been export led in the sense that Japan has developed globally competitive industries. This contrasts with growth policies seeking to expand primarily with import-competing industrial substitution, as tried in Latin America. Import substitution policies end up misallocating resources by producing goods in which a country has a comparative disadvantage. However, the Japanese have not developed their export industries much faster than total output.

Japanese exports will increase by fifty times over the forty-year period from 1955 to 1995 (as measured in constant 1988 dollars). Exports were $8.9 billion in 1955 and are estimated at $450 billion in 1995. This is an annual rate of growth in exports of 10.3 percent per annum over this period. From table 1.1 we saw that the GNP growth rate over this period was 9.5 percent, going from $103 billion to $3,897 billion, or a thirty-eight–fold increase. Exports of goods have thus increased from 8.6 percent of GNP in 1955 to an estimated 11.5 percent of GNP in 1995. As we saw in table 1.1, Japanese exports of goods and services increased from 13 percent of GNP to 16 percent of GNP in 1985 and are estimated to fall back to 14 percent of GNP by 1995.

The other countries listed in table 1.1 experienced more rapid increases in the ratio of exports to GNP than did Japan. Japan's increase is only 1 percent of GNP, going from 13 percent to 14 percent. This is an increase of 8 percent in the ratio of exports to GNP, which can be considered to be a measure of dependency of a country on export markets for the maintenance of its GNP. Japan was 8 percent more dependent on exports in 1995 than in 1955. The U.S. share of exports went from 4 percent of GNP in 1955 to 13 percent in 1995. This is an increase of 225 percent in export dependence. West Germany will go from exports being 20 percent of GNP in 1955 to 42 percent of GNP in 1995. This is an increase of 110 percent in export dependency. Mexico is expected to increase its exports to GNP ratio from 15 percent in 1955 to 20 percent in 1995. This represents a 33 percent increase in export dependency. Of the four countries examined, Japan had the lowest change in its export to GNP ratio. This would hold true even if Japan does not reduce this ratio from the 16 percent level of 1985, as it is expected to do.

Table 2.1
Japanese Exports by Major Trading Partners

	1955	1965	1975	1985	1995[a]
United States					
Value of Exports	$2,038	$9,008	$23,038	$72,246	$153,000
Country's Share of Japan's Exports	.23	.30	.20	.38	.34
Japan's Share of Country's Imports	.04	.11	.12	.20	.21
West Germany					
Value of Exports	$112	$772	$3,394	$7,639	$27,000
Country's Share of Japan's Exports	.01	.03	.03	.04	.06
Japan's Share of Country's Imports	.004	.01	.01	.05	.05
China					
Value of Exports	$129	$879	$4,618	$13,652	$31,500
Country's Share of Japan's Exports	.01	.03	.04	.07	.07
Japan's Share of Country's Imports	NA	NA	NA	.31	.33
South Korea					
Value of Exports	$178	$646	$4,599	$7,791	$22,500
Country's Share of Japan's Exports	.02	.02	.04	.04	.05
Japan's Share of Country's Imports	.15	.36	.33	.24	.26
Hong Kong					
Value of Exports	$392	$1,033	$2,821	$7,150	$18,000
Country's Share of Japan's Exports	.04	.03	.02	.04	.04
Japan's Share of Country's Imports	.14	.17	.21	.23	.25
United Kingdom					
Value of Exports	$272	$736	$3,010	$5,190	$18,000
Country's Share of Japan's Exports	.03	.02	.03	.03	.04
Japan's Share of Country's Imports	.01	.01	.03	.05	.05
Australia					
Value of Exports	$245	$1,123	$3,560	$5,887	$18,000
Country's Share of Japan's Exports	.03	.04	.03	.03	.04
Japan's Share of Country's Imports	.02	.09	.18	.23	.25
World					
Value of Exports	$8,937	$30,334	$114,073	$192,436	$450,000
Japan's Share of World's Exports	.02	.05	.06	.09	.10

Source: United Nations, *Yearbook of International Trade Statistics,* various years.

Note: Dollar figures are in millions of 1988 dollars.

[a] Estimated.

Exports by Country

The perception of Japan as an aggressive, "export at any price" trade partner, while not valid from an objective standpoint, is understandable. Residents of various countries see Japanese goods accounting for increasing shares of their goods markets and they become alarmed. Looking at table 2.1, we can see that Japan has had a steady increase in its share of total world exports. Japan exported 2 percent of the value of world exports in 1955. Japan's share had risen to 9 percent by 1985, and is expected to rise to 10 percent by 1995.

The United States' relative openness to Japanese goods can be seen in 1955 and later periods. Japan's share of the U.S. import market in 1955 was 4 percent, or double its share of world exports. In 1985 its share of the U.S. import market was 20 percent, which is a little more than double Japan's 9 percent share of the world's exports in 1985. Thus, Japan's increasing share of the U.S. market has paralleled its increasing share of the global market. Japan's share of global exports excluding the United States would be much higher, since the United States has been the world's largest exporter during this period.

Japan's share of the imports of West Germany and the United Kingdom has grown, but is still much smaller than its share of world exports. Japan's share of West Germany's imports was only 1 percent in 1975, and grew to 5 percent by 1985. It is probable that part of the explanation for the low share in Germany is the presence of trade barriers on Japanese exports to the European Economic Community. Of course, another explanation is that Japan's and Germany's relative costs of production are similar. This would cause them to export and import roughly the same kinds of goods. In this case they would not trade much with each other. We will examine trade barriers to Japanese exports in chapter 4.

China, South Korea, Hong Kong, and Australia import relatively large amounts of Japanese goods. In 1985, Japan's share of China's import market was 31 percent, 24 percent in South Korea, and 23 percent in Hong Kong and Australia. These shares are two and a half to more than three times the share of Japan in global exports. Part of the explanation lies in Japan's comparative advantage in the commodities these countries want to import. Part of the explanation is that Japan has relatively low transportation costs to these countries, since they are all in the Pacific area. In addition, these countries lack preferential agreements, such as in the EEC, that divert imports away from the most efficient producer. Again, this will be an issue when we look at barriers to Japanese exports in chapter 4.

Table 2.1 also shows each country's share of Japan's exports. This reveals the relative importance of the individual country's market to Japanese exporters. It is clear from the table that the United States is the most important market for Japan. The United States was least important to Japan in 1975, and even then it was 20 percent of Japan's total export market. Presently, the United States accounts for 38 percent of Japan's export market. The decline in the relative position of the United States in Japan's exports was primarily due to the first oil shock. Saudi Arabia and other oil-exporting countries represented a much higher portion of Japan's export market in 1975 than in 1965. Their higher incomes allowed them to sharply increase their imports. By 1985, the oil-exporting countries had suffered substantial losses in their purchasing power as the real price of oil fell. The United States had allowed an overvalued dollar to draw sharply higher imports from most countries including Japan in 1985. My estimate for 1995 is for the U.S. share to fall to 34 percent of Japan's exports. This is due to slower growth in U.S. imports as the United States tries to correct its trade deficit.

The other countries included in table 2.1 are much less important as markets for Japanese goods. China received 7 percent of Japanese exports; West Germany, South Korea, and Hong Kong each received 4 percent; and the United Kingdom and Australia each received 3 percent. I estimate a small increase by 1995 in the shares of West Germany and the United Kingdom, due in part to reduction in trade barriers. I am also estimating a small increase in the share of Japanese exports going to South Korea and Australia. This is primarily due to the relative growth of those countries' imports and the slowdown in U.S. imports. I am assuming that Japanese exports to China will remain at the same relative level as 1985 (7%), although clearly this will depend on policy developments in the early 1990s.

Exports by Commodities

Economic theory predicts that a country will export those goods in which it has a comparative advantage. Table 2.2 shows the pattern of Japanese exports by broad commodity categories (one-digit categories of the Standard International Trade Categories or SITC). These categories have been established by the United Nations for classifying goods in international trade. The categories with the largest share of Japan's exports should be those categories in which Japan has a comparative advantage. Interpreted in this way, the change in shares over time would reflect changes in Japan's comparative advantage.

In 1955, 58 percent of Japan's exports were in basic manufactured goods such as steel, steel products, rubber products, etc. Only 12 percent of exports were in machinery and transportation equipment. Over the years, the percentage of Japan's exports in basic manufactured goods has declined to 16 percent in 1985, and it is expected to decline to 10 percent in 1995. This does not simply reflect a change in global output of basic manufactured goods. In Organization for Economic Cooperation and Development (OECD) countries as a whole, exports of basic manufactured goods increased slightly faster than total exports from 1964 to 1987. The ratio went from .404 to .408 (OECD, 1989). So, Japan's comparative advantage shifted away from basic manufactures during this period.

Japanese exports in machinery and transportation equipment have increased to 68 percent of total exports in 1985, and are expected to go to

Table 2.2
Japanese Exports by Commodity Category

		1955	1965	1975	1985	1995[a]
All Exports (millions of 1988 dollars)		$8,937	$30,334	$114,073	$192,436	$450,000
SITC Rev. 2	Commodity Category	Share of Exports				
0	Food & Animals	.07	.04	.01	.01	.01
1	Beverages & Tobacco	.00	.00	.00	.00	.00
2	Crude Materials Except Fuel	.05	.03	.01	.01	.01
3	Fuels	.00	.00	.00	.00	.00
4	Animal & Vegetable Oils	.01	.00	.00	.00	.00
5	Chemicals	.05	.06	.07	.04	.03
6	Basic Manufactured Goods	.58	.40	.31	.16	.10
7	Machinery & Transportation Equipment	.12	.31	.49	.68	.74
8	Miscellaneous Manufactures	.13	.14	.08	.09	.10
9	Other Goods	.00	.01	.01	.01	.01

Source: United Nations, *Yearbook of International Trade Statistics,* various years.

[a] Estimated.

74 percent in 1995. This is more than a six-fold increase in the percentage of total exports in machinery and transportation equipment since 1955. Machinery and transportation equipment manufacturing uses a relatively large amount of capital and professional and technical workers (Qureshi, Strangways, and Turner, 1986). So, it is not surprising to see Japan exporting heavily in this area, since they have moved to a greater abundance of capital and professional workers. However, basic manufacturing, which has decreased in relative importance for Japan, is even more capital-intensive. Part of the explanation must lie in the rapid growth of industries in the machinery and transportation equipment area.

Machinery and transportation exports went from 30 percent to 41 percent of total exports for the OECD countries as a whole from 1964 to 1987 (OECD, 1989). This is about a 35 percent increase in the ratio. Machinery and transportation exports for the OECD countries were expanding at a faster pace than exports as a whole. Because of Japan's rapid growth and high savings and investment rates, it was able to direct resources into this high-growth area. Japanese exports of machinery and transportation equipment increased at a very rapid rate as a result.

Japan has never had a significant share of exports in beverages and tobacco, fuels, animal and vegetable oils, or other miscellaneous goods. Exports of miscellaneous manufactures have ranged from 8 percent to 14 percent of total exports, with no definite time trend. Likewise, the share of chemicals in exports has ranged from 3 percent to 7 percent without a clear time trend. Exports of food, animals, and crude materials besides fuel have declined as a share of total Japanese exports. The decline has been from 7 percent to 1 percent and from 5 percent to 1 percent, respectively. This is what we would expect from Japan's growing relative abundance of capital and professional work force. Those commodities using relatively little of these factors are less likely to be exported.

Machinery and transportation equipment appears to be an area of greater innovation than other commodity categories. There is more scope for rapid adjustment, market positioning, and various strategic behaviors in this area than in more established commodity categories. As a consequence, some of Japan's success in this area is due to the fact that it was growing very rapidly over this period. If a significant part of total capital is new, then it is likely to be such innovative areas that are perceived (probably correctly) as having high future rewards. In short, a greater portion of Japan's capital will be utilized in areas with bright prospects from a global perspective because much of its capital is recently acquired. Other countries also allocate their new investment to those industries that look most promising at the time of investment. However, the rate of investment in most other countries is not as high as it is in Japan. Consequently, they are not likely to be able to exploit global growth opportunities to the same degree that Japan can. This global growth effect is in addition to the increased output in machinery and transportation equipment that one would expect due to Japan's increasing capital and technical personnel per worker.

Exports by Commodity and Country

Table 2.3 shows Japanese exports by Japan's most important export categories to some of its most important trading partners for the year 1987. The commodity categories presented here by three-digit SITC constitute 45 percent of Japan's exports in 1987. The remaining 55 percent were distributed over three-digit categories having less than $5 billion in Japanese exports for the year 1986. In addition to dollars of exports in the category to a particular country, table 2.3 shows the distribution of the share of Japanese exports in the particular category over the listed countries. Also shown is the share of imports from Japan in each country's total imports for the listed commodity categories. Lastly, table 2.3

lists the share of the particular commodity category in Japan's total exports; this is only shown for the world total.

As we saw in table 2.2, 68 percent of Japanese exports are in the one-digit SITC category 7, machinery and transportation equipment. Table 2.1 showed Japanese exports by country of destination. Both of these tables reported results over time. Table 2.3 provides information on the most important commodity categories at a more detailed level. All three-digit SITC codes with more than $5 billion dollars of Japanese exports in 1986 are included in table 2.3. This represents all categories with more than 3 percent of Japanese exports in 1986. The exports are reported by SITC number and country of destination.

Presenting the data in this way allows us to see which commodity exports are most important to Japan. We also can analyze which countries are the most important markets for Japanese goods and whether this importance varies by commodity class. We can also analyze how important Japanese goods are in the import markets of the various countries. From this we can gain some understanding of possible comparative advantage and/or the existence of trade barriers.

Table 2.3 reports the following data:

1. Japanese exports in millions of current dollars by commodity category and country of destination;
2. the share of the country in Japan's exports of the particular commodity;
3. the share of Japan's exports of this particular commodity in this country's total imports of this particular commodity; and
4. the share of this commodity in Japan's total exports for 1987.

Data is presented for all exports, SITC 674 (iron and steel), and for seven subcategories of machinery and transportation equipment.

Without exception, the United States is the most important market for Japan's exports in these commodity categories. The United States' share of Japan's exports in the various commodity categories in table 2.3 varies from 20 percent in iron and steel to 60 percent in passenger cars. The second-lowest share for the United States was in transistors (26%), and the second-highest was in automatic data processing equipment (51%). The commodity area with the largest Japanese exports to the United States was passenger cars, with $21.4 billion in 1987. Overall, the United States was the destination for 37 percent of Japan's exports in 1987. This ratio is very close to the share of the United States in the GNP of the global economy excluding Japan. In 1985, the United States had 41 percent of non-Japanese global GNP (United Nations, *Yearbook of National Accounts Statistics*).

Table 2.3
Japanese Exports by Country and Commodity, 1987

SITC Rev. 2		United States	West Germany	South Korea	Hong Kong	United Kingdom	World
All	Total Exports	$84,232	$12,832	$13,214	$8,865	$8,400	$229,054
	Share of Japan's Exports	.37	.06	.06	.04	.04	1.00
	Share of Country's Imports	.21	.06	.33	.19	.06	.09
	Commodity's Share of Japan's Exports						1.00
674	Iron & Steel Sheet	$ 1,206	$ 30	$ 501	$ 190	$ 5	$ 6,078
	Share of Japan's Exports	.20	.00	.08	.03	.00	1.00
	Share of Country's Imports	.33	.02	.88	.58	.01	.25
	Commodity's Share of Japan's Exports						.03
752	Automatic Data Processing Equip.	$ 4,735	$ 1,119	$ 239	NA	$ 650	$ 9,375
	Share of Japan's Exports	.51	.12	.03	NA	.07	1.00
	Share of Country's Imports	.49	.20	.46	NA	.12	.21
	Commodity's Share of Japan's Exports					.04	
763	Sound Records & Phonographs	$ 4,038	$ 660	$ 105	$ 331	$ 381	$ 8,593
	Share of Japan's Exports	.47	.08	.01	.04	.04	1.00
	Share of Country's Imports	.74	.68	.91	.66	.41	.62
	Commodity's Share of Japan's Exports						.04

764	Telecommunications Equipment	$ 4,623	$ 1,055	$ 549	$ 432	$ 789	$ 12,461
	Share of Japan's Exports	.37	.08	.04	.03	.06	1.00
	Share of Country's Imports	.44	.42	.74	.40	.32	.32
	Commodity's Share of Japan's Exports						.05
776	Transistors	$ 2,136	$ 497	$ 1,146	$ 755	$ 393	$ 8,312
	Share of Japan's Exports	.26	.06	.14	.09	.05	1.00
	Share of Country's Imports	.27	.18	.49	.34	.18	.21
	Commodity's Share of Japan's Exports						.04
781	Passenger Cars	$21,422	$ 2,793	NA	NA	$1,169	$ 35,693
	Share of Japan's Exports	.60	.08	NA	NA	.03	1.00
	Share of Country's Imports	.46	.33	NA	NA	.15	.28
	Commodity's Share of Japan's Exports						.16
782	Lorries	$ 4,292	$ 74	NA	NA	$ 151	$ 8,596
	Share of Japan's Exports	.50	.01	NA	NA	.02	1.00
	Share of Country's Imports	.54	.05	NA	NA	.14	.30
	Commodity's Share of Japan's Exports						.04
784	Motor Vehicle Parts	$ 5,171	$ 129	$ 470	NA	$ 495	$ 10,955
	Share of Japan's Exports	.47	.01	.04	NA	.05	1.00
	Share of Country's Imports	.29	.06	.69	NA	.08	.17
	Commodity's Share of Japan's Exports						.05

Source: United Nations, *Yearbook of International Trade Statistics, 1987.*

Note: Dollar figures are in millions of current dollars.

If we consider trade of differentiated products, a pure model would imply each country's commodities are different from every other country's. In this instance, the benefits of trade come from having wider choices of goods because of trade. A country's exports would be distributed according to the income of its trading partners. This is in contrast to the pure comparative advantage model, where countries would only export certain commodities and only import certain other commodities. Real world trade patterns reflect both types of trade.

SITC categories 781, 782, and 784, comprising cars, trucks, and parts, constitute 25 percent of Japanese exports. Exports to the United States in these categories range from 47 to 60 percent of Japan's exports in these categories. This is substantially in excess of the 41 percent share of non-Japanese global GNP. One explanation would be that the United States had a substantial comparative disadvantage in producing these products. However, this does not seem very plausible in view of the relatively strong position of the United States in world automotive production. Part of the explanation lies in the higher number of automobiles per GNP in the United States. Part of the reason is the high value of the dollar in the mid-1980s. Another reason, however, is the presence of substantial barriers to Japanese exports of cars to members of the EEC. These high-income countries, which otherwise would be expected to import a lot of Japanese cars, manage to restrict those imports to a relatively low level (Shepherd, 1982).

Export Dependence

Japan is frequently characterized as being export dependent or export driven. Certainly, exports are important to Japan's economy, but upon examination of the relevant data, it is clear that Japan's export dependence has been exaggerated. Most of Japan's output is not exported. As indicated in table 1.1, only 16 percent of Japanese GNP was exported in 1985. Table 2.4 is designed to show export dependence at the industry level. It is possible for a country to export a low percentage of its output overall, but to export virtually all of the output of certain key industries. The industries selected for inclusion in table 2.4 were those three-digit ISIC categories where Japan exported 10 percent or more of total supply in 1985.

The data in table 2.4 reveal a general increase in the level of Japan's export performance. This largely reflects a global trend over this period of greater exchange of goods internationally. For all the OECD countries, export performance for manufacturing increased from 12.2 percent in 1970 to 17.0 percent in 1985, which represents the same percentage

Table 2.4
Japanese Exports of Manufactures as a Percentage Share of Total Supply: Export Performance Ratios

ISIC		1970	1975	1980	1985
3--	Manufacturing	9.6	12.4	13.2	14.6
321[a]	Textiles	16.1	14.9	15.2	14.1
323[a]	Leather Products	11.4	12.2	11.3	12.0
351[a]	Industrial Chemicals	12.0	17.6	12.2	12.1
355	Rubber Products	12.9	17.2	17.1	17.1
361	Pottery, China, & Earthenware	28.8	25.0	26.8	25.6
371	Basic Iron & Steel	16.5	28.8	21.5	18.9
382	Non-Electric Machinery	9.4	16.2	20.7	25.9
383	Electric Machinery	14.0	18.8	23.7	25.4
384	Transport Equipment	17.9	30.9	33.0	36.5
385[a]	Professional & Scientific Equipment	18.3	23.3	29.3	30.0

Sources: Berthet-Bondet, Blades, and Pin (1988); Brodin and Blades (1986).

[a] These categories also appear in Table 3.4 as industries with relatively high import penetration.

growth as experienced by Japan. In 1985, Japan's export performance for manufacturing was 14.6 percent, which was lower than the 17 percent for all of OECD. It was much lower than Germany's 35.8 percent export performance in manufacturing, although it is higher than the 6.8 percent rate of the United States.

The three-digit ISIC category with the greatest relative change in Japan's export performance was nonelectric machinery (ISIC 382). The level of export performance went from 9.4 percent to 25.9 percent. This is an increase of 1.76 times over this fifteen year period. Pottery, china, and earthenware's export performance declined over this period from 28.8 percent to 25.6 percent, as did textiles, which declined from 16.1 percent to 14.1 percent. Export performance for leather products, industrial chemicals, and basic iron and steel remained relatively flat during this fifteen year period. Transport equipment had the highest export performance at the end of the period, at 36.5 percent. Professional and scientific equipment was second in export performance, at 30.0 percent.

SUMMARY

Japanese exports from 1955 through 1985 reflect Japan's dynamic growth. Japan has become much more important as a supplier to the global market. Japan is an especially important exporter to the United States and the Pacific Rim countries. Japan has become a major exporter of machinery and transportation equipment. Its role as a supplier of basic manufactured goods has become less important. There have been significant changes in Japan's comparative advantages. Japan now concentrates more on producing goods with relatively skilled labor inputs as well as high capital intensity.

Japan appears to have strategically developed export markets. Its major exports today are in the areas of differentiated products, which include automobiles and consumer electronics. It has used the growth of its economy to seize the lead in areas of rapid growth in the global economy. Nevertheless, Japan's exports have not outpaced its growth in GNP to the extent that we have seen in most other countries in the postwar period. Many of the trade adjustments forced on its trading partners come from Japan's rapid economic growth.

3 JAPANESE IMPORT PATTERNS

Japanese import patterns are a good example of comparative advantage. Most Japanese imports fall into the categories of crude materials and fuels. These two broad categories represented 62 percent of Japanese imports in 1955, and 57 percent in 1985. Throughout the postwar period crude materials and fuels have represented the bulk of Japanese imports. These are the commodities that use factors of production such as land and natural resources, which are scarce in Japan. Consequently, they would be very expensive to produce in Japan if there were no trade with the rest of the world. As Japan's income continues to grow, there should be some increase in imports of differentiated manufactures and some decrease in the portion of crude materials in imports.

Between the years 1955 and 1985, the United States has been the largest provider of Japanese imports. The U.S. share of Japan's imports was 22 percent in 1987, and is likely to rise to 25 percent by 1995. The United States exports food and agricultural commodities, aircraft, aluminum, coal, and many other goods to Japan. Saudi Arabia, the United Arab Emirates, and Indonesia are principal suppliers of petroleum to Japan. Petroleum has the largest value share in Japan's imports, at 15 percent, in 1987.

Japanese imports of manufactured goods are the lowest, as a share of apparent consumption, of any of the advanced industrial countries. Japan imported only 5.3 percent of its manufactured goods consumed in 1985. The average for all the countries in the Organization for Economic Cooperation and Development (OECD) was 19.5 percent. This is an area where Japan's trading partners, especially the United States, are pressuring Japan to import more.

WHY COUNTRIES IMPORT

To understand the import patterns of any country in the global economy, it is imperative that we first understand why countries import and the effects of such imports. The simplest way to understand imports is from the position of a consumer. When we decide what items to purchase, we consider all items in the marketplace that fulfill our particular need. We consider all the relevant characteristics of such a commodity, including price. We select the commodity that has the best array of characteristics for a given price or, alternatively, we select the commodity with the lowest price that has the characteristics we desire.

As an individual consumer, we take the price as given. Of course, if we are in a bazaar where the price is subject to haggling, we may not take the price as given. Even then, we would not enter into haggling unless the price we expected to pay would make us interested in buying the product. But generally speaking, we take the price as given in deciding among the various alternatives available. So, looking at the whole range of consumer goods and the prices of those goods, we will purchase the item that gives us the greatest satisfaction for the amount of our expenditure.

For instance, if we are considering the purchase of a car, we would look at all the relevant characteristics of a car. How fast can it go? What gas mileage does it get? What colors are available? How quickly does it accelerate? Does it maintain its resale value? What are the likely maintenance requirements? Does it have a good stereo? And, of course, how much does it cost?

We select the car that has the best array of characteristics and price as far as our personal preferences and budget are concerned. The comparison of commodities by characteristics is very complex and personal. We can gain assistance from various automotive reports, dealer ads, showroom visits, and so forth. Nevertheless, whether we prefer a car that accelerates from zero to sixty in twelve seconds or one that gets thirty-five miles per gallon depends on individual preference as well as knowledge of the product. For example, I do not really care how quickly an automobile accelerates, but I do like it to get relatively good gas mileage. Alternatively, another person might care more about acceleration than gas mileage.

Economists focus on price in the decision of the consumer. Partly this is to avoid mathematical complexity. By focusing on price, we are developing a framework of analysis that reveals how supply and demand for commodities and factors of production interact. We can then use this analysis to illuminate how interactions in the more complicated real world will tend to work out in the long run. Most students of international trade theory seem to believe the development of trade models with simple uniform commodities is complicated enough.

It is important, however, when considering the real world, to be aware that economic models are a simplification. Frequently, we need to change our assumptions and models to highlight the aspect of the real world that is of the greatest concern for a particular project. Here, we assume away all of the differences in characteristics among the commodity, and consider price alone. We are assuming that all goods are homogeneous. This assumption would imply that you cannot tell one car from another. However, since this abstraction from the characteristics of automobiles is so removed from reality because cars are the epitome of differentiated products, we will consider a bolt of cloth as the import good. We know that bolts of cloth differ from one another, but at least it is easier to imagine a world in which all bolts of cloth are the same than one in which all automobiles are the same.

If all bolts of cloth are the same, the consumer would then choose on the basis of price. Hence, with the characteristics of the bolts of cloth, foreign and domestic being the same, the prices will be the same. Sometimes this is referred to as the "Law of One Price." It is not so much a law of observed patterns as a law based on logical deductions once the assumption of homogeneity of the product is made.

As consumers, we choose the product that has the lower price. When we are looking for commodities that are imported into a country, there are a number of possibilities, but the basic relationship has to be that if the commodity were not imported it would be cheaper in the foreign country than the locally produced commodity. The cheapness is in terms of relative prices. The relative price of cloth is how much of other commodities we have to give up to get another bolt of cloth. Of course, this does not mean that the imported commodity has to be cheaper at the free market equilibrium. In fact, if you assume away the differences in commodities, the price of the imported commodity and the domestically produced commodity will be the same in the domestic market after trade takes place. If trade did not take place, the price would be higher at home than in the foreign economy. We import more of those commodities that are relatively cheaper to produce abroad. Next, let us look at what economists call general equilibrium effects of trade.

When we import a commodity from the rest of the world, the price of the commodity will tend to rise in the rest of the world and fall in the domestic economy. Imports are not purchases made just by an individual consumer. Rather, we are looking at the economy-wide purchase of foreign goods. We are aggregating over all consumers, all private firms, and all government agencies. In short, we are looking at all buyers in the society.

As more is purchased from foreign suppliers, the tendency is for the price to rise. This is because of either of two basic relationships. One is the standard assumption of an upward-sloping supply curve. More of a commodity will be supplied by a firm or industry only if a higher price is offered. The second relationship is the effect of higher input prices on commodity prices. If all firms in the export industry of a foreign economy increase output, the prices of the inputs to the production process of that particular product will rise. The prices of those inputs will rise and cause the firms in that industry to raise the price at which a particular amount of the commodity will be offered for sale. The supply curve will have shifted. As we import more, assuming that we are large enough to affect world prices, the import's price will increase.

Economists have very elaborate models, such as trade offer curves, that are used to look at different relationships between prices and the quantity of a good offered for export or the amount of a good that a country will want to import. Without getting into the technical aspects of that analysis, the general tendency is for an increase in the demand for a commodity to cause an increase in the price of that commodity in the global market, everything else being equal. Of course, as we know, everything else is not equal. Things are changing all the time. That makes the process of estimating these relationships fairly difficult.

We know the price of the commodity that our country imports would be lower in the global market than in our own economy if our country did not participate in trade. As we tend to buy some of the commodity for import, it will tend to raise the price of the commodity in the rest of the world. The opposite happens in the domestic market. That is, as we import more of the commodity, the domestic price will fall. This is because the quantity of the domestically produced good demanded at a given price will now be lower, due to the availability of imports. Suppliers will only be able to produce and sell their output at a lower relative price than prevailed without trade. The price in the domestic economy will tend to be driven down as we import more from abroad. The amount of the import-competing good produced in the domestic economy will be lower than it would be if we were in isolation.

Thus, two price effects from importing work in opposite directions. We have the price of the import good rising in the global market. We also have the price of the good falling in the home market because of our imports. Of course, given our assumption that you cannot tell one bolt of cloth from another, the price of the foreign and domestic good will be identical in the home country after trade reaches some equilibrium level. If there were no barriers to trade, the price would be the same in the domestic and foreign economy.

If we do not make the assumption of homogeneity, the general price effects will still tend to be the same, but prices of foreign and domestic goods will not, in general, be identical. If foreign and domestic goods are different from each other, then when we import a commodity, the demand for similar domestic goods will be reduced. This will tend to cause the price and quantity produced of goods closely substitutable with the import good to fall. The final equilibrium price of the domestic goods can be lower or higher than the import good.

Let us use cars as an example of a heterogeneous commodity. If Japan imports more cars from the United States, the result will be to cause the price of cars and profits in the U.S. auto industry to rise. Similarly, the imports of cars from the United States will tend to keep prices of cars in Japan lower than they would be otherwise. These price effects are most pronounced for those cars that are closest in style and purpose to the imported cars. If Japan imports luxury cars, their prices will be much higher than most Japanese models. The relative price of the imported and domestic car will depend on the various characteristics of the car and costs of production and distribution. Market share will depend on price and these various attributes.

In general, the lower the price of the import good, the larger will be its share of the market for the relevant commodity class. The more we import, in this context, the higher the global price of the import commodity is likely to be, for the same reasons as offered above for homogeneous commodities.

What, then, is the benefit of importing? For a given money income, it is easy to see the benefits of importing. The price of the imported good with trade is lower than it would be domestically without trade. Hence, consumers could buy more goods with the same income and so would be better off.

Of course, money income does not stay the same. Nevertheless, in a perfectly competitive economy, production will adjust to maximize real income. Trade causes changes in production toward producing more of the higher-priced exports and less of the lower-priced imports. Economists can demonstrate that, even with no change in production, the society can benefit from trade. With production changing, the potential benefits from trade are enhanced. It is as though money income increases at the same time that prices are reduced. The consumption possibilities of the economy are greater with free trade. No trade is inferior to free trade.

We know there are gains, or at least potential gains, from trade. Generally, trade causes change in relative prices. Such price changes usually cause some groups to be better off and some groups to be worse off. What economists can demonstrate is that trade with redistribution could make some groups better off without making anyone worse off. If the winners from trade compensated the losers, there would still be some gains remaining. If such compensation does not take place, then the potential gain is present, but we cannot definitely say the country has gained from trade.

The gains from trade might be captured by a portion of the population. This may or may not make the whole country better off. It depends on the relative merits of the groups winning and losing. The tendency, if you are in the group that loses, is to claim that trade is bad, even if some other groups gained more than your group lost.

Such distributional gains, while important, are essentially an internal political issue on how to share the national gains from trade. However, if such political issues are not addressed to the satisfaction of ruling groups in the society or to the satisfaction of the electorate, then free trade may not be permitted even though potential benefits would accrue.

The firms in the import-competing industries and the owners of resources used in those industries are the groups that tend to be adversely affected by international trade. This includes laborers in those industries if their skills are not freely usable in export industries. This is because of the squeeze in production by these firms as imports increase. Production will be lower than without imports. Consequently, these firms and groups are usually the ones promoting protectionist policies. Such protectionism may be bad for the country, but it is good for these affected groups.

When we look at a country's import pattern, we expect to find a country importing commodities that are relatively less expensive to produce abroad than at home. Of course, most commodities are not homogeneous, especially manufactured goods. We have commodities that are, instead, relatively substitutable. They may be substitutable in function, for instance, but they are not identical. Sometimes they can be very different, like a Honda Civic versus a Cadillac Seville. Other times they are not as different, but importantly so, such as the difference between a half-inch bolt and a twelve-millimeter bolt.

JAPANESE IMPORTS

Our examination of the pattern of Japanese imports is similar to our examination of Japanese exports. First, we will look at the major commodities that Japan imports. This is because Japan's import commodities largely determine the countries exporting to Japan. Next, we look at the major countries exporting to Japan. Then, we look at major import categories and the major countries that are sources for those categories. Lastly, we look at the ratio of Japanese imports to Japanese consumption in selected commodity categories.

Imports by Commodity

Looking at Japan's import patterns, we expect to find heaviest imports in those areas where it would be very expensive for Japan to produce the

Table 3.1
Japanese Imports by Commodity Category

		1955	1965	1975	1985	1995[a]
All Imports (millions of 1988 dollars)		$11,016	$29,319	$118,392	$141,716	$450,000
SITV Rev. 2	Commodity Category	Share of Exports				
0	Food & Animals	.25	.17	.14	.11	.12
1	Beverages & Tobacco	.01	.01	.01	.01	.02
2	Crude Materials Except Fuel	.50	.39	.20	.14	.10
3	Fuels	.12	.20	.44	.43	.37
	(33) Petroleum & Products	.09	.16	.36	.31	.28
4	Animal & Vegetable Oils	.01	.01	.00	.00	.00
5	Chemicals	.03	.05	.04	.06	.08
6	Basic Manufactured Goods	.02	.07	.06	.08	.10
7	Machinery & Transportation Equipment	.05	.09	.07	.08	.10
8	Miscellaneous Manufactures	.01	.02	.03	.05	.07
9	Other Goods	.00	.00	.00	.03	.04

Source: United Nations, *Yearbook of International Trade Statistics,* various years.

[a] Estimated.

commodity. The extreme case is where Japan could not produce the commodity at any price. It is a common perception that Japan imports raw materials and exports manufactures. To a large degree, this perception is, in fact, correct. Japan's imports are heavily weighted in raw materials including fuels.

Japanese import patterns are a good example of comparative advantage. As shown in table 3.1, most Japanese imports fall into the categories of crude materials and fuels. These two broad categories represent 62 percent of Japanese imports in 1955, 59 percent in 1965, 66 percent in 1975, and 57 percent in 1985. So throughout the postwar period, Japanese imports have been heavily weighted in those commodities that are relatively expensive or impossible to produce in Japan.

There has been some increase in imports recently in categories with differentiated products. Chemicals, basic manufactured goods, machinery and transportation, and miscellaneous manufactures include such differentiated products. This increase in imports of differentiated products is partly due to the income effect. As Japan's income has grown, its total demand for manufactures has increased sharply because of the higher income elasticity of demand for these goods. Some of this increased demand has fallen on foreign goods, thus increasing imports.

Table 3.1 was constructed to show how Japan's imports have changed over the period from 1955 to 1985, and how they might change to 1995. The first line of table 3.1 shows the total of all imports by Japan in millions of 1988 dollars. This gives us a rough guide to the real increases in the level of Japanese imports. Japan's imports increased from $11 billion in 1955 to $142 billion in 1985, and are expected to increase further to $450 billion by 1995.

As previously discussed, a large portion of the increase in dollar amounts between 1985 and 1995 is caused by the fall in the value of the dollar. In 1985, the yen/dollar exchange rate was 239, and by 1990 it was 150. Imports costing a Japanese purchaser one million yen in 1985 and 1995 would be worth $4,184 at 239 yen/dollar and $6,667 at 150 yen/dollar. Thus, the same value in yen would cost 59 percent more in dollars.

The dramatic increase of Japanese imports from 1955 to 1985 of more than twelve times indicates the degree to which Japan's economy has grown. Japan's imports have grown rapidly as its economy grew. Japan is a much more powerful force in the global economy today than it was in 1955.

Finally, table 3.1 shows the shares of various commodity categories as a portion of Japan's total imports for various years. Standard International Trade Classification (SITC) one-digit commodity categories are used in these calculations. Observations are given for 1955, 1965, 1975, and 1985, and 1995 estimates are provided. For instance, commodity category 0, food and animals, declines from .25 in 1955 to .11 in 1985. This represents a trend of decline in Japan's relative imports of food and animals. This reflects the relatively low income elasticity of demand for food and animals. Houthakker and Magee (1969) showed that the income elasticity of demand for U.S. exports of food was .51, while income elasticity for exports was 1.07 for U.S. manufactures. So, as Japan's income has increased, the relative expenditure on imports of food and animals has tended to decline. Since Japan's increase in income has been rapid, so has the relative decline in imports of food.

A numerical example may make the elasticity effect on food imports clearer. If we use the U.S. export elasticities as proxies for Japan's import demand elasticities, we can calculate the effect of Japan's increased income on the share of food in imports. In 1955, food and animals are 25 percent of Japan's imports, and manufactures (SITC 6, 7, and 8) are 8 percent. By 1965, Japan's real income had tripled, or increased by 200 percent, from its 1955 level. With an income elasticity of .51, Japan's imports of food would increase by .51 × 200 percent, to 102 percent. Imports of manufactures, with an income elasticity of 1.07, would increase by 1.07 × 200 percent, to 215 percent.

If all other imports had an elasticity of 1.0, they would increase proportionately to income, or 200 percent. In this hypothetical case, where we are ignoring all changes in prices or tastes, Japanese imports in 1965 would look like this:

Food	1955 level + 1.07 × 1955 level
Manufactures	1955 level + 2.14 × 1955 level
Other Goods	1955 level + 2.0 × 1955 level

The approximate 1955 level of food imports was $2,754 million in 1988 dollars ($11,016 × .25). The approximate 1955 level for manufactured imports was $881 million ($11,016 × .08), and all other imports was $7,381 million ($11,016 × .67). Substituting these values into the equations for the level of 1965 imports, we obtain estimates for the level of imports in 1988 dollars for 1965. These are

			Shares of total
Food	$ 2,754 + 2,947	= $ 5,701	.19
Manufactures	881 + 1,885	= 2,766	.09
Other Goods	7,381 + 14,762	= 22,143	.72
Total	$11,016	$30,610	

Comparing these hypothetical effects with the actual changes observed, we note that the predicted income effects are largely borne out in reality. Japanese imports in 1965 reached the level of $29,319 million, which is very close to the predicted level $30,610 million. Food and animals were 17 percent of imports instead of the predicted 19 percent. Manufactures were 18 percent instead of 9 percent. In other words, Japan's imports of manufactures grew more rapidly than expected, looking at income alone. Nevertheless, the general pattern of a lower share of food imports as Japan's income increases is observed.

Beverage and tobacco products have stayed at approximately 1 percent over our period of observation. It is expected that Japan's liberalization of trade in tobacco and beverages might raise this category to 2 percent by 1995. Even so, it will remain a very small portion of Japan's total imports.

SITC category 2, crude materials except fuel, has accounted for a substantial portion of Japan's total imports. It has ranged from 50 percent of Japan's imports in 1955 to 14 percent in 1985. It is expected to decline further to about 10 percent by 1995, as Japan increases its imports of consumer goods and other manufactures. Also, crude materials tend to be a lower portion of the value of output in the types of goods Japan produces today compared to the mix of Japanese output forty years ago. This also shows up in the relative decline in Japan's exports of basic manufactured goods, which was discussed in chapter 2. Nevertheless, this still constitutes one of the major areas of Japanese imports.

Table 3.1 also shows the share of fuel (SITC 3) in Japan's imports. The following item listed in the table is petroleum and products (SITC 33). The difference between these two shares is largely coal imports. As can be seen, the fuel share ranges from a 12 percent share in 1955 to a 44 percent share in 1975. The share declined to 43 percent in 1985, and is expected to decline further to a 37 percent share in 1995. This still will be by far the largest share of Japanese imports in any one-digit SITC category. The expected decline is based on the expected stability of fuel prices in dollars and the continuation of a yen that is much stronger against the dollar than it was in 1985. Iraq's invasion of Kuwait may change this expectation. It certainly has raised oil prices in the third quarter of 1990. Japan has also increased the efficiency of fuel utilization in automobiles and manufacturing. Fuel imports as a share of Japan's imports will also tend to fall as Japan increases its imports of more finished goods.

The categories of chemicals, basic manufactured goods, machinery and transportation equipment, miscellaneous manufactured goods, and other goods generally represent differentiated products. As Japan's income comes closer to and indeed exceeds that of other advanced industrialized economies, we should expect its imports of these differentiated goods to increase. All of these categories have been estimated to have some increase in import share from 1985 to 1995. Such increases range from 1 to 2 percent of import share.

Basic manufactured goods' import share ranges from 2 percent in 1955 to 8 percent in 1985. It is expected to be 10 percent in 1995. Machinery and transportation ranges from an import share of 5 percent in 1955 to 9 percent in 1965, and has since fallen to 8 percent in 1985. Of course, as we saw in chapter 2, this is an area of Japanese export advantage and represents the largest share of Japanese exports. Thus, it is not surprising to see a fairly small share of Japanese imports in this area. Miscellaneous manufactures' share has ranged from 1 percent in 1955 to 5 percent in 1985. This shows a rapid rate of increase in this category, but it remains a modest portion of Japan's total imports. Other goods (SITC 9) have been less than 1 percent of Japanese imports, except in 1985. Animal and vegetable oils have been 1 percent or less of Japanese imports in all periods.

What can we conclude from the information presented in table 3.1? Japan has indeed tended to import heavily in the areas of crude materials and fuels. This is what we would expect based upon comparative advantage and the relative factor abundance of Japan. As we saw in table 1.1,

Japan has a lower abundance of land and its associated natural resources than the other countries we looked at. Relative to most countries in the global economy, Japan's land per 1,000 workers is at the low end of the spectrum. Consequently, we would expect it to be very expensive for Japan to extract crude materials and fuels. In an isolated Japan, these goods would have a very high equilibrium price. So, these are the commodities that Japan imports in large amounts. Japan's import pattern thus confirms comparative advantage as a powerful explanatory theory.

Table 3.2
Japanese Imports by Major Trading Partners

	1955	1965	1975	1985	1995
United States					
Value of Imports	$3,452	$8,492	$23,756	$28,318	$112,500
Country's Share of Japan's Imports	.31	.29	.20	.20	.25
Japan's Share of Country's Exports	.04	.08	.09	.11	.15
Saudi Arabia					
Value of Imports	$437	$520	$12,560	$11,208	$31,500
Country's Share of Japan's Imports	.04	.02	.11	.08	.07
Japan's Share of Country's Exports	NA	.20	.20	.24	.28
Indonesia					
Value of Imports	$361	$535	$7,018	$11,070	$31,500
Country's Share of Japan's Imports	.03	.02	.06	.08	.07
Japan's Share of Country's Exports	.08	.16	.44	.47	.50
Australia					
Value of Imports	$794	$1,981	$8,511	$7,993	$31,500
Country's Share of Japan's Imports	.07	.07	.07	.06	.07
Japan's Share of Country's Exports	.08	.17	.30	.26	.34
China					
Value of Imports	$361	$808	$3,137	$7,092	$22,500
Country's Share of Japan's Imports	.03	.03	.03	.05	.05
Japan's Share of Country's Exports	NA	NA	NA	.21	.25
Canada					
Value of Imports	$486	$1,281	$5,113	$5,149	$18,000
Country's Share of Japan's Imports	.04	.04	.04	.04	.04
Japan's Share of Country's Exports	.02	.04	.07	.05	.09
World					
Value of Imports	$11,016	$29,319	$118,392	$141,716	$450,000
Japan's Share of World's Imports	.03	.04	.06	.06	.10

Source: United Nations, *Yearbook of International Trade Statistics,* various years.

Note: Dollar figures are in millions of 1988 dollars.

[a] Estimated.

Imports by Country

Table 3.2 is developed to show the primary countries that provide Japanese imports. These countries should generally have a comparative advantage at exporting those commodities that Japan most wants to import. The results show some of the interconnections between countries in the global economy. The table presents data on the value of Japanese imports from various countries in constant 1988 dollars for the years 1955, 1965, 1975, and 1985, and estimates for 1995. The level of Japan's imports from each country is also presented as a share of Japan's total imports and as a share of the exporting country's total exports. The former ratio shows how important a country is as a provider of goods to Japan. The latter figure shows how important Japan's market is to the particular exporting country.

The countries in their order of importance as providers of Japanese imports are the United States, Saudi Arabia, Indonesia, Australia, China, and Canada. The total value of Japanese imports is also reported for the world as a whole in constant dollars. More interestingly, this value is also reported as a share of world imports.

The United States provided 20 percent of Japan's imports in 1985. There is a downward trend in imports from the United States over the 1955–85 period. In 1955, the United States provided 31 percent of Japan's imports. In 1965, 29 percent of Japan's imports were provided by the United States. The percentage dropped to 20 percent in 1975, largely as a shift in the value of all imports due to the sharp rise in oil prices in 1974. The U.S. share remained low in 1985 due to the overvaluation of the dollar, which tended to reduce the competitiveness of U.S. goods in global markets. The U.S. share of world exports had declined in 1985 as a result of the dollar valuation. This effect was not limited to Japan.

In 1985, Saudi Arabia and Indonesia each supplied about 8 percent of Japanese imports. Saudi Arabia's exports to Japan are virtually all crude petroleum and petroleum products. Indonesia provided substantial amounts of petroleum products, but also exported other goods in substantial amounts to Japan. Australia provided 6 percent of Japanese imports in 1985. It provided many crude materials to Japan including energy, mostly coal. It also provided foodstuffs to Japan. Some manufactured goods are also provided to Japan by Australia, but not a great deal.

China provided 5 percent of Japanese imports in 1985; Canada provided 4 percent. Total Japanese imports in 1985 were $141.7 billion (1988 dollars). This was 6 percent of total world imports in 1985. Japanese imports were only 3 percent of world imports in 1955.

As can be seen, the United States has experienced a decline in its share of Japanese imports. We expect the United States' share to increase from 1985 to 1995. This is due to the devaluation of the dollar since 1985, which makes U.S. goods more competitive in Japanese markets. Indeed, the lower value of the dollar will make U.S. goods more competitive in all global markets. The United States' share of all markets should increase as a result.

Devaluation is slow to work in increasing share, however. This is because the devaluation of the dollar is roughly equivalent to lowering the price of all U.S. exports and raising the price of U.S. imports. If the quantities of exports and imports did not change, the value shares of U.S. exports would actually decline. It is only if the percentage increase in quantity is greater than the percentage decrease in price in nondollar currency, that the U.S. share would increase.

Other exports that had roughly constant dollar prices would be affected the same way by the dollar devaluation. Considered from the Japanese perspective, the decrease in the dollar's value from 1985 has drastically lowered the price of their imports of oil and other dollar-denominated imports of crude materials. The price of oil fell in dollar terms and then it fell another 50 percent in terms of yen because of the dollar devaluation before the dollar strengthened some. In mid-1990, the dollar was 37 percent lower in value than it was in 1985.

The United States has also been pressing Japan on various liberalization measures, especially on goods in which the United States has a comparative advantage (*The Wall Street Journal*, February 23, 1990, p. A-1). Overall, Japan has been responding with increased imports from the United States in a fairly dramatic way. The United States should have its share of Japanese imports rise to 25 percent or so by 1995.

The other major changes in the shares of Japanese imports that we see in table 3.2 are the increased shares of Saudi Arabia and Indonesia. Between 1965 and 1975, Saudi Arabia's share of Japanese imports went from 2 percent to 11 percent. Indonesia's share of Japan's imports was 2 percent in 1965, and went to 6 percent in 1975. Of course, this was primarily due to the dramatic rise in the price of oil in the 1973–74 period.

The other countries have had relatively stable shares of Japanese imports. China's share did rise from 3 percent in 1955 and 1965 to 5 percent in 1985, due to its increased participation in world commerce.

The share of Japan in the exports of the various countries shows a more consistent pattern. There are impressive increases in Japan's share of each country's exports over this period. For the United States, Japan had a 4 percent share of exports in 1955. This share increased to 8 percent in 1965, 9 percent in 1975, and 11 percent in 1985. It is expected to increase further to 15 percent in 1995. This shows the increasing importance to the United States of Japan as an export market.

The same pattern of increasing importance of Japan as an export market generally holds for the other countries as well. Japan's share of Indonesia's exports went from 8 percent in 1955 to 47 percent in 1985.

Japan received 8 percent of Australia's exports in 1955 and 26 percent in 1985. Japan imported 2 percent of Canada's exports in 1955 and 5 percent in 1985. This reflects Japan's more rapid growth than the rest of the world. As Japan grows, it imports more and since it grows faster, its imports grow faster as well. Japan is simply becoming more important as an export market for most countries in the global economy.

Imports by Commodity and Country

Table 3.3 shows Japan's imports by country and by commodity. This is presented for the single year 1987, the latest year for which U.N. statistics are available. Table 3.3 presents data on Japanese imports by major three-digit SITC categories from the United States, Saudi Arabia and United Arab Emirates, Indonesia, Australia, and the world as a whole. This provides additional detail on comparative advantage and interrelationships between Japan and its major import suppliers. The three-digit categories reported are shellfish, coal, petroleum, petroleum products, pharmaceutical products, aluminum, and aircraft.

For each three-digit SITC category the value of Japanese imports from the particular country is reported. The share of Japan's imports from each country in each listed import category is also reported. Then, the share of the country's exports in the category that goes to Japan is reported. For the world as a whole, the share of the three-digit category in Japan's total imports is reported.

As an example of how to read the table, we can look at SITC 036, shellfish. We can see that $204 million of shellfish were exported from the United States to Japan in 1987. This was 5 percent of Japan's imports of shellfish in 1987. Japan received 61 percent of all the shellfish exported by the United States in 1987. Japan received 83 percent of the shellfish exported by Indonesia, and 56 percent of the shellfish exported by Australia. In total, Japan received 39 percent of all shellfish exported in the world. Shellfish imports were 3 percent of the total value of Japanese imports in 1987.

Without discussing all of the individual line items in the table, some interesting points can be noted about this data. For the United States, Japan does not account for an extremely large share of its export market, except for shellfish, where Japan received 61 percent of the U.S. exports. The United States is a critical supplier of aircraft to Japan (90%), and a major supplier of pharmaceuticals (30%). Saudi Arabia and the United Arab Emirates are critical sources of Japan's crude petroleum and petroleum products (41 and 30%, respectively). Japan, in turn, is of major importance to them as an export market, receiving 32 percent of their crude petroleum and 43 percent of their petroleum products.

Table 3.3
Japanese Imports by Country and Commodity, 1987

SITC Rev 2		United States	Saudi Arabia & UAE	Indonesia	Australia	World
All	Total Imports	$31,691	$11,152	$8,427	$7,368	$146,048
	Share of Japan's Imports	.22	.08	.06	.05	1.00
	Share of Country's Exports	.11	.26	.45	.24	.06
	Commodity Share					1.00
036	Shellfish	$ 204	NA	$ 309	$ 207	$ 3,947
	Share of Japan's Imports	.05	NA	.08	.05	1.00
	Share of Country's Exports	.61	NA	.83	.56	.39
	Commodity Share					.03
322	Coal	$ 584	NA	$ 14	$2,158	$ 4,648
	Share of Japan's Imports	.13	NA	.00	.46	1.00
	Share of Country's Exports	.14	NA	.28	.49	.31
	Commodity Share					.03
333	Crude Petroleum	NA	$8,287	$2,673	NA	$ 20,140
	Share of Japan's Imports	NA	.41	.13	NA	1.00
	Share of Country's Exports	NA	.32	.52	NA	.15
	Commodity Share					.14
334	Petroleum Products	$ 469	$2,105	$ 908	NA	$ 7,089
	Share of Japan's Imports	.07	.30	.13	NA	1.00
	Share of Country's Exports	.18	.43	.74	NA	.11
	Commodity Share					.05
541	Pharmaceutical Products	$ 669	NA	NA	$ 4	$ 2,110
	Share of Japan's Imports	.32	NA	NA	.00	1.00
	Share of Country's Exports	.20	NA	NA	.04	.08
	Commodity Share					.01
684	Aluminum	$ 380	NA	NA	$ 551	$ 2,669
	Share of Japan's Imports	.41	NA	NA	.08	1.00
	Share of Country's Exports	.30	NA	NA	.54	.14
	Commodity Share					.02
792	Aircraft	$1,579	NA	NA	$ 37	$ 1,755
	Share of Japan's Imports	.90	NA	NA	.02	1.00
	Share of Country's Exports	.10	NA	NA	.01	.07
Commodity Share						.01

Source: United Nations, *Yearbook of International Trade Statistics, 1987.*

Note: Dollar figures are in millions of 1988 dollars.

Australia and Indonesia are closely tied by trade to Japan. In 1987, Japan received 45 percent of Indonesia's exports, and 24 percent of Australia's exports went to Japan. Japan received 49 percent of Australia's coal exports, which accounted for 46 percent of Japan's coal imports. Over half (54%) of Australia's aluminum exports went to Japan. Japan received 52 percent of Indonesia's exports of crude petroleum, and 74 percent of Indonesia's petroleum products exports. It is clear that any disruption of Indonesian-Japanese trade would have a devastating impact on Indonesia's economy. On the other hand, Japan is not as dependent on Indonesia as a source of its imports, receiving only 6 percent of its overall imports from Indonesia.

Import Penetration

Table 3.4 shows how important imports are in specific manufacturing industries in Japan. The data reported are import penetration ratios in percentage terms. The import penetration ratio is defined as imports divided by the sum of production and the difference between imports and exports of a particular good category. The divisor in this ratio is referred to as "apparent consumption," since production plus imports minus exports indicates how much is available for usage in the importing country. Low figures for import penetration ratios indicate that a particular industry is largely free from import pressure. Large numbers indicate that foreign suppliers provide a substantial portion of the goods in a particular industry.

The data come from the Organization for Economic Cooperation and Development (OECD) Compatible Trade and Production Data Base (Berthet-Bondet et al., 1988; Brodin and Blades, 1986). The industry categories are all in manufacturing, and are given for all three-digit International Standard Industrial Classification (ISIC) categories with more than 8 percent import penetration ratios for Japan. These categories thus represent Japanese manufacturing industries that face the most foreign competition in the Japanese market.

The import penetration ratio for Japan's manufacturing industry as a whole ranges from 4.7 percent in 1970 to 5.8 percent in 1980. The ratio declined to 5.3 percent in 1985. This ratio is the lowest for all the OECD countries. The next-lowest ratio reported for the twenty-two OECD countries was Yugoslavia, at 10 percent. The United States was the third lowest, at 12.9 percent. West Germany, another major industrial country like the United States and Japan, had an import penetration ratio for manufacturing of 38.7 in 1985.

It is clear that Japan's import penetration ratio in manufacturing is very low. One reason for Japan's low import penetration ratio is that it has a comparative advantage in manufacturing. If all industrial goods were homogeneous (perfect substitutes), then Japan probably would not import manufactures at all. With heterogeneous goods being produced, there is strong competition among various brands of the same kind of good. Consequently, it is expected that different brands will be sold in each market around the world. This kind of trade in differentiated prod-

Table 3.4
Japanese Imports of Manufactures as a Percentage Share of Apparent Consumption: Import Penetration Ratios

ISIC		1970	1975	1980	1985
3--	Manfacturing	4.7	4.9	5.8	5.3
311	Food Manufacturing	8.5	8.6	9.8	7.3
321[a]	Textiles	4.1	6.1	7.6	8.3
322	Wearing Apparel	4.4	8.3	13.8	16.5
323[a]	Leather Products	6.0	9.2	11.9	12.2
324	Footwear	2.4	6.3	10.2	12.0
331	Wood & Cork Products	4.7	6.5	9.1	9.2
351[a]	Industrial Chemicals	7.1	7.0	9.3	11.5
353	Refined Petroleum Products	14.9	8.6	10.3	8.0
372	Non-Ferrous Metals	16.7	16.6	20.2	18.9
385[a]	Professional & Scientific Equipment	7.6	9.4	9.6	8.7

Sources: Berthet-Bondet, Blades, and Pin (1988); Brodin and Blades (1986).

[a] These categories also appear in Table 2.4 as industries with relatively high export performance.

ucts is called intra-industry trade, and a large share of international trade is of this type (see Grubel and Lloyd, 1975). The low import penetration ratios for Japan have led critics of Japan to conclude that Japan discriminates against foreign manufactures. This issue will be discussed further in chapter 5. Japan does have barriers to imports of manufactures. However, its barriers are not distinctly worse than those of other countries.

The import penetration ratios for different three-digit categories reported in table 3.4 range from 2.4 percent for footwear (ISIC 324) in 1970 to 20.2 percent for non-ferrous metals (ISIC 372) in 1980. In 1985, they range from 7.3 percent for food manufacturing (ISIC 311) to 18.9 percent in non-ferrous metals. There is a general trend toward higher import penetration ratios over this period, but it is not very pronounced.

The ratio for Japan's manufacturing industry increased by 12.7 percent from 1970 to 1985, going from 4.7 percent to 5.3 percent. The ratio for the OECD countries as a whole increased by 57.3 percent over the same period, going from 12.4 percent to 19.5 percent. The sharpest increase in the ratios shown in table 3.4 was for footwear, which increased by 400 percent, going from 2.4 percent in 1970 to 12.0 percent in 1985. The next sharpest increase is in wearing apparel (ISIC 322), which increased 275 percent, going from 4.4 percent in 1970 to 16.5 percent in 1985. These industries, as well as textiles, leather products, and wood and cork products, are basic industries, an area where Japan's comparative advantage is receding. We saw in chapter 2 that Japan's share of exports in these industries is decreasing over time. This shift is also reflected in the higher import penetration ratios in these basic industries as time proceeds. Japan's higher levels of capital and professional and technical labor power are shifting Japan's comparative advantage to more advanced industrial products.

Four of the industries listed, textiles, leather products, industrial chemicals, and professional and scientific equipment, also appeared in table 2.4. These categories thus have a substantial amount of imports and exports. We can characterize them as having heterogeneous products and intra-industry trade. An unweighted average of their import penetration ratio was 6.2 percent in 1970. It rose to 10.2 percent in 1985, which is an increase of 64.5 percent. Whether this increase is due to higher Japanese income, the change in comparative advantage, or liberalization of Japan's trade policies and practices, it represents substantial progress in an area of importance for Japan's trading partners.

I have estimated a measure similar to that reported in table 3.4 for coal and lignite from data in the *Japan Statistical Yearbook* (various years). The ratio calculated is imports divided by total demand for coal and lignite. In 1955, imports were 6.4 percent of demand, increasing to 25.1 percent in 1965, 76.1 percent in 1975, and 84.1 percent in 1985. So, domestic output of coal fell from 93.6 percent of total demand for coal in 1955 to only 15.9 percent in 1985. This fairly dramatic rise in the import penetration ratio for coal can be explained both by Japan's rapid rise in output with a greater need for energy sources, and by liberalization of import quotas on coal, which is discussed in chapter 5. Japan has not produced and does not produce a significant amount of petroleum, so the import penetration ratio there is practically 100 percent.

SUMMARY

The Japanese economy could almost be considered a case study in the benefits of international trade. Japanese imports largely reflect the operation of trade by comparative advantage. The Japanese import goods that would be very expensive to produce in Japan if it were a closed economy. These import goods are mostly fuel, crude materials, and food and agricultural goods, which together accounted for 68 percent of Japan's imports in 1985.

The United States is by far the most important exporter to Japan. In

1985, the United States supplied 20 percent of Japan's imports. U.S. exports to Japan cover a wide range of goods, from agricultural commodities to jumbo jets. Japan only received 11 percent of the U.S. exports in 1985. Thus, even though Japan is very important to the United States both as a supplier of imports and as a market for exports, the United States remains much more important to Japan. This is one reason that the United States has been able to exert so much negotiating pressure on Japan in the bilateral trade talks that take place from time to time.

Other countries that are important suppliers of Japan's imports are Saudi Arabia, Indonesia, Australia, China, and Canada. Indonesia is most closely tied to Japan as a market, with 47 percent of its exports going to Japan. Australia and Saudi Arabia provide 26 percent and 24 percent of their exports to Japan. Indonesia's shellfish and petroleum goods go primarily to Japan. Canada exports less than 10 percent of its goods to Japan.

Japan does not import a large portion of its apparent consumption of manufactured goods. This result is consistent with comparative advantage, since manufacturing is where Japan can produce at a low cost relative to other goods. Manufacturing is characterized by intra-industry trade in most advanced countries. As Japan continues to grow in income and liberalizes trade, it is likely to increase the proportion of manufactures it imports.

4 TRADE BARRIERS TO JAPANESE EXPORTS

We often think of Japan as a country that restricts imports, since it has been running large trade surpluses for a number of years. The value of Japan's exports is much greater than the value of its imports. Many commentators do not consider the restrictions placed on Japanese exports. It is the stated policy of the United States, Japan, and other members of the Group of Seven (Canada, France, Germany, Italy, and the United Kingdom) to reduce Japan's trade surplus. The Group of Seven is an informal association of the largest free market oriented countries. They hold meetings of central bankers, finance ministers, and chief executives to coordinate economic policies. The focus of most analysis is, therefore, how and why Japan's exports are so large and why Japanese imports are not larger. Measures designed to reduce Japanese import barriers are put forward as ways to reduce Japan's present trade surplus. In this chapter, however, we examine the measures that have been taken against Japan's exports.

There have been more restrictions placed on the exports of Japanese goods during the postwar period than on any other major country's exports. The reasons are manyfold, but certainly a major cause has been the rapid economic growth in Japan. We have seen that Japan's growth in production has caused its share of world output to increase considerably. Since rapid growth in an export industry also tends to lower the relative price of the export, this means Japan's rapid growth has caused a fall in prices of the goods Japan exports. This in turn threatens to disrupt non-Japanese producers, who then seek relief against Japan.

International economic trade theory demonstrates that rapid growth in a country such as Japan will tend to lower the country's terms of trade. This fall in the relative price of Japan's exports has a number of effects. First, it limits the potential welfare benefits to Japan of its rapid growth. Theoretically, it would be possible for a country's export industry to grow so much and its export prices to fall so far that the country is actually worse off because of growth. This is called "immiserizing growth" (see Caves, Frankel, and Jones, 1990, p. 61). Immiserizing growth has not happened in the case of Japan, but falling relative prices of its exports have. Japan's welfare would have been greater if its own growth in industries like video cassette recorders and camcorders did not cause the price to fall. It is, however, the nature of the competitive marketplace that not all the benefits of change accrue to the initiator of change.

A second effect of lower prices of Japanese exports due to rapid growth is the increase in consumer welfare in those countries that import Japanese goods. As the prices of Japanese goods fall, consumers demand more of such goods. This increase in consumer welfare coming from being able to buy more of all goods is a primary benefit of free trade or relatively free trade.

A third effect of the falling prices of Japanese exports is the negative impact on producers of similar goods in the rest of the global economy. As the price falls, producers will see their profits shrink and will tend to cut output of such similar products. If the Japanese price falls far enough, producers in most countries can be driven out of the business altogether. When output is cut back, people are laid off, machinery must sometimes be scrapped, and distress is widespread in the industry competing with Japanese exports.

It is this third effect of falling prices due to Japan's rapid growth that has led to strong protectionist measures against Japan. At various times Japan's exports have faced special tariffs, special quotas, and so called "voluntary export restraints" designed to protect the domestic industries of Japan's trading partners. Such barriers are in addition to those trade barriers facing most other trading partners. Japan has often been singled out for special discriminatory protectionist measures.

Politically, it is sometimes possible to bring about trade policies that are not in the national interest. When an industry is in distress due to imports from Japan or some other country, it is easy to define the loss in terms of lost jobs, reduced output, and negative profits. Furthermore, the losses are concentrated within a distinct group of firms and workers. This makes it relatively easy to organize and affect the political agenda.

The domestic winners from Japanese trade are a more diffuse group. Consumers will be able to buy at a lower price or will have a superior product. Exporters in the domestic economy will sell more to Japan and other countries because of higher export earnings in Japan. When Japan exports to country A, it "earns" foreign exchange that it will spend on imports. Some of these imports come from country A. Other imports will come from country B. However, country B's exports to Japan will allow it to buy more goods from country A. This also is a widely diffused effect. It does not matter which goods we import. They all tend to increase our level of exports in the long run. Because of the asymmetry in the magnitude of effects between beneficiaries of trade and those harmed, the political process tends to favor those advocating protectionist measures (Baldwin, 1981).

One of the most visible effects of distress in an import-competing industry is the loss of jobs in the industry. Such job loss is politically more objectionable when unemployment in the economy is at a high level (Neumann, 1981). It is during periods of recession and large trade deficits that we hear the loudest calls for protectionism. In the short run, restricting imports increases aggregate demand and will increase employment. However, when we restrict imports to increase employment at home, it reduces foreign exports and employment in the foreign country. If foreign countries retaliate, then our exports fall and unemployment increases at home. This kind of "beggar your neighbor" protectionism was tried during the 1930s, and is held partly to blame for the world-wide depression of that era (Kindleberger, 1986).

Unemployment policy is best pursued with other macroeconomic measures that are not so disruptive to foreign economies and inviting of retaliation. Highly restrictive trade policies and liberal trade policies are both consistent with full employment and balance of payments equilibrium. In the long run, though, with full employment and free trade, all countries participating in the global economy will be more prosperous because their citizens will enjoy a higher standard of living.

EFFECTS OF TRADE BARRIERS

There are many different effects of various trade barriers. They raise the price of the import commodity. This reduces the amount of imports and increases the domestic output of the competing domestic good. Consumers are harmed by the results. Firms and workers producing the export-competing good are benefited, at least in the short run. Firms and workers producing goods for export are harmed. The government may obtain some tariff tax revenue depending on the nature of the trade barrier. These effects will be explained in detail for a tariff imposed on an import commodity that is perfectly substitutable for a domestically produced good. Other situations with imperfect substitution of commodities and different kinds of trade barriers will be briefly explained.

Tariffs

When a tariff is imposed on imports, a tax is paid when the good is imported. Whatever the price of the commodity in the world market, the price in the domestic market will be higher than that, because an importer will have to pay the cost of the good plus the tax. If there is no difference between the domestic good and the import, then the domestic good's price will also have to equal the world price plus the tariff.

If the importing country's market is large relative to the global market for the good, then imposing a tariff is likely to affect the world price. This effect is due to the reduction in the quantity of imports demanded because of the tariff. Assuming a rising industry supply curve, the reduction in demand results in a lower relative price. If the tariff is imposed by a country with a large market for the taxed good, the world price of the good will be lower relative to the prices of other goods as a consequence.

The reduced demand for imports in the country imposing the tariff comes from both a reduced quantity of the import good demanded and an increase in the quantity supplied by domestic producers. The amount of the good imported at a given price is simply the amount by which demand exceeds supply. The demand for imports is simply excess demand in the country's market at various prices. When the domestic price rises due to the tariff, domestic consumers will buy a smaller quantity. On the other hand, domestic suppliers are willing to supply more because of its higher price. Excess domestic demand is less at the higher, tariff-ridden, price.

The willingness of domestic producers to supply more of the import good at the higher price because of the tariff is a reflection of economic incentives. If no additional output is provided at the higher price, then economic profits will accrue to existing firms producing in the industry. It is this possibility of higher profits that leads to the new level of output. Each firm in the industry can earn more profit by expanding output even if it has an upward-sloping marginal cost curve (the cost of producing one more unit increases as output expands). Further, in a perfectly competitive industry, there are no barriers to entry. Thus, new firms would enter the industry and increase output of the industry even if existing firms did not increase output. In such a perfectly competitive world, profits are quickly reduced to a normal level. This eliminates excess or economic profits. If competition is not so fierce, then excess profits will accrue to firms in the industry.

If firms in the industry do expand output, they have to attract factors of production (workers and capital) from other uses. This shift in production leads to changes in relative prices of the factors of production. Stolper and Samuelson (1941) showed that the changes in the relative prices of the factors of production are greater than the percentage changes in relative prices of the commodities. Prices rise for those factors of production that are used intensively in the production of the commodity whose relative price rises. In the case of a tariff being imposed, the imported commodity has an increase in price. This leads to an even greater increase in the price of factors intensively used to produce the import good.

In the short run, any worker in the import industry is likely to gain from imposing a tariff, because of increased demand in that particular industry. However, if the export and nontradeable industries are more labor intensive, when they reduce output, wages will fall relative to the factor returns for the factor used intensively in the import industry. In the long run, at any given level of unemployment, the increased output in the import-competing industry has to cause a decline in the production of other industries.

The consumer of the import good is clearly harmed by imposing a tariff. As a result of the tariff, the consumer must pay a higher price for the good. The consumer thus pays a higher price and consumes less of this commodity than before. The extent to which we value consumer purchases more than the price we pay is called consumer surplus. If our tastes and income are unchanged, we lose consumer surplus whenever price is increased. A tariff reduces consumer surplus. Consumers are the primary losers from tariffs.

As we saw, import-competing firms and factors gain from the tariff. They capture some of the consumer surplus lost by consumers. Their gain is considered an increase in producer surplus.

The government also gains some revenue by imposing a tariff. There will be tariff revenue equal to the amount of imports times the tariff amount on each unit. Consumers lose more than the sum of producer surplus and tariff revenue. The extra loss or deadweight loss of social welfare is due to inefficiencies in our social choices of how much to produce and consume, because the tariff-ridden domestic cost of the import good is not its true opportunity cost. Without the tariff, we would produce less and consume more. At a given world price, the society loses when a tariff is imposed.

There are only three ways for a society to gain by imposing a tariff. The first is by redistribution. If society views the transfer from consumers and exporters to producers in the import industry as desirable even though the consumers lose more, then the tariff could be considered a gain. Of course, other more efficient ways of making such a transfer could be devised.

The second possible gain from imposing a tariff comes from the fall in the world price of the import good. This is a change in the import country's terms of trade that will tend to improve its welfare. It is similar to keeping money income constant, and reducing the price of some of the goods you normally buy. It is possible for this gain to be large enough to more than offset the loss from distorting the domestic market. This has sometimes been suggested to lower the price of oil in the world market. Most objections to Japan's exports, though, have been that Japanese prices are too low, not too high. This improvement in the importing country's welfare comes at the expense of the exporting country. If our terms of trade improve, then their terms of trade must deteriorate.

A third possible gain from imposing a tariff is to increase employment and output when the importing country is in recession. This has been discussed before. However, there are domestic policies than can be used to accomplish the same goal. Further, if the importing country increases output by reducing imports, its trading partners are likely to suffer unemployment as a consequence. Movement of labor and other resources in and out of industries is expensive. Temporary changes should not be encouraged.

Even though society could gain from imposing tariffs, it seems clear that, more than likely, society as a whole loses when a tariff is imposed. If our country does gain by imposing a tariff, it is almost surely at the expense of our trading partners. If they impose barriers on our exports in retaliation, then we both lose. Some workers and firms are likely to gain at the expense of consumers and the export industry.

Imperfect Substitution and Tariffs

If a tariff is imposed on imports where goods are similar but not identical, the general results are the same, but some steps are different. The initial impact of the tariff on the foreign import is the same. The domestic producers will see an increase in the demand for their goods when import prices go up. If the domestic industry is competitive, then output and prices will increase as before. The only difference is that the equilibrium price would not necessarily be the same as that of the foreign import. If the domestic industry is not competitive, then the increased demand caused by the tariff will increase industry profits. Output may not change very much. It will depend on where the oligopolistic industry can achieve its best profits. Workers in the oligopolistic industry may be able to capture some of the oligopoly rents as a reward for politically supporting the tariff. The consumer still loses the most.

Quotas

Quotas are quantitative limits on the amount of imports that will be allowed into the country. In a competitive economy, we can calculate a tariff that would have an effect equivalent to a particular quota. This tariff equivalent would result in the desired level of imports being exactly equal to that allowed by the quota. Quotas in a monopolistic or oligopolistic setting do not have an exact tariff equivalent. This is because a quota allows more room for continued monopoly behavior than a simple tariff does. A tariff that results in the same level of imports as a quota is likely to cause lower, more competitive, pricing among firms in the domestic import-competing industry.

A quota also results in the equivalent of tariff revenue accruing to the entity holding the right to import under the quota. This tariff-equivalent revenue will only go to the government if the import rights are sold to the highest bidder. This is seldom done. Sometimes the tariff-equivalent revenue goes to the traditional importer and sometimes it goes to import-competing producers. The right to import under a quota can be of considerable value.

Voluntary Export Restraints

"Voluntary export restraints" (VERs) have been used extensively in limiting Japan's exports. VERs are limits placed on a country's exports by the country of export. They are "voluntary" in the sense that the exporting country agrees to restrain exports. Usually, this agreement is entered into because more burdensome provisions are threatened by the importing country if agreement is not reached. It is somewhat like saying a bank teller volunteers to hand over the bank's money when a robber is pointing a gun at the teller. Such "voluntary" action is better than the probable alternative.

VERs have roughly the same effects as discriminatory tariffs, with the tariff revenue accruing to the exporting country. It is discriminatory because exports from the country agreeing to the restraint are treated differently from exports from other countries. There is some tariff which could be applied to imports from the restraining country that would result in just the agreed-upon level of imports. This is the tariff equivalent of the VER. Since the restraint is usually imposed by the exporting country, it can more properly be considered to have an export tax equivalent. Again viewed from this perspective, it would be a discriminatory export tax. It would not apply equally to all export markets (see Turner, 1983).

The economic rents that accrue from VERs generally go to exporters. Since fewer exports can be made to a market, prices in that market are generally higher as a result. Since costs of production reflect the prices that would have prevailed in the market with free entry, the higher price under the restraint represents additional revenues. When the exporting country is restricting exports, these extra revenues accrue to the exporter. In the case of Japan, explicit export cartels were often formed to facilitate the administration of the VER (Turner, 1983, pp. 795–96). The extra revenue accruing to the exporters from the VER is one reason an exporting country prefers to institute VERs than to have quotas imposed.

Regulatory and Other Nontariff Barriers

Regulatory barriers to trade are among the most persistent and perverse nontariff barriers. Such barriers are very difficult to identify because they are usually said to exist for other reasons, such as the furtherance of health and safety of the public. Yet they are frequently used to restrict and sometimes prohibit foreign imports. Establishing national standards can be used to improve technological progress, or to deliberately restrict foreign penetration of the domestic market. It is difficult to tell when standards and regulations are legitimate and when they are mainly barriers to trade.

Regulatory measures also tend to be very harsh. They tend to exclude certain imports that do not meet requirements. As such, they have tariff equivalents that are extremely high, since the effect is that of a prohibitive tariff. The barriers to trade posed by such measures are higher than could be justified using a tariff.

Nontariff barriers have other real costs attached to them. Resources have to be used by firms to figure out what regulations exist, what permission to import has to be obtained, and from whom. Government resources are involved in administering quotas and VERs and in setting and supervising regulations. In some countries, the required permissions result in large-scale graft and corruption of administering agencies. But, even in the best of situations, there are delays and uncertainties because of the nontariff barriers. Due to these factors, tariff restrictions resulting in the same level of imports are superior to a system of nontariff trade barriers in most cases.

Modern production requires a long planning horizon for efficient allocation of resources. Firms might spend years in the development of a new product, and development of a production line and marketing strategies takes additional time. The investment in plant, equipment, and training of workers usually requires years of production before profitability is enough to cover the initial investment. This indicates how important it is to have relative stability in the global trading system if firms are going to produce for the global market. Moreover, it is production for the global market by the most efficient global producers that ensures the highest well-being of consumers and workers around the world. This is why it is so important that barriers to trade be kept in check by the world's policy makers.

TRADE NEGOTIATIONS AND TARIFFS FACING JAPAN

Japan has participated with other countries in a series of multilateral trade negotiations under the auspices of the general commercial policy section of the International Trade Organization (ITO). The International Trade Organization was intended to be a strong international agency to move the international trading regime toward freer trade following World War II. The U.S. Congress did not ratify the treaty to establish the International Trade Organization. The commercial policy section of the ITO was adopted. It consists of a set of rules regarding trade and is known as the General Agreement on Tariffs and Trade (GATT). However, GATT did not develop the strong directorate that was originally intended (Baldwin, 1984). Nevertheless, a number of GATT conferences have been held since 1947. The Uruguay Round is continuing at the present time. It is the eighth round of GATT talks aimed at reducing trade barriers.

Table 4.1 presents estimates of the levels of tariffs imposed by Japan's trading partners at selected times since 1930. Also presented in table 4.1 are estimates of the tariff equivalents of nontariff barriers facing Japan's exports in the 1980s. Column E presents the estimated 1987 tariff levels facing Japan. The earlier columns in the table (A–D) show the tariff levels in various industrial categories under the assumption that all tariffs were cut proportionately in all the GATT negotiating rounds. In fact, all tariffs were not cut proportionately, but it is virtually impossible to get accurate estimates of tariff levels in earlier periods (Curtis and Vastine, 1971, p. 228). The estimates should be considered as order of magnitude guesses, but they do tend to show the changes that have helped to expand the level of world commerce. Such changes have contributed enormously to the economic prosperity in the postwar period.

The 1987 tariff levels (after the 1974–79 Tokyo Round of GATT talks) shown in column E are based on the work of Deardorff and Stern (1986), as reported in Saxonhouse and Stern (1989). Saxonhouse and Stern present tariff levels for various countries weighted by their own levels of imports. This has the convenience of being able to use tariff revenue summations and dividing by the sum of imports to get average tariffs for various categories. This was also the approach taken by Turner (1981 and 1989) for aggregating nontariff barrier tariff equivalents. It has the disadvantage of underweighting extremely high trade barriers. Since high trade barriers result in very low imports, an extremely high tariff on a particular commodity would get little weight in this procedure.

Constructing a level of tariffs facing a particular country such as Japan is even more complicated than showing tariffs imposed by a particular country. One approach would be to take each country's tariff level for an industry and weight it by the level of imports from Japan. Of course, such an approach would be very data intensive, that is, it would require an awful lot of work. When completed, it would still have the disadvantage of underweighting very high barriers. I took the simpler expedient of giving 50 percent weight to the U.S. tariff level, since the United States is Japan's most important trading partner. France and Germany's tariff

Table 4.1
Tariffs and Tariff Equivalents of Other Trade Barriers to Japanese Exports

ISIC	Industry Category	1930 Tariffs (A)	1955 Tariffs (B)	1965 Pre-Kennedy Tariffs (C)	Pre-Tokyo Tariffs (D)	1987 Tariffs (E)	1987 Nontariff Barriers (F)	Tariff[a] Revenue (G)	Tariff[a] Revenue Equiv. (H)
1--	Agriculture, Forestry, & Fisheries	15.6	7.8	7.3	4.7	3.2	3.8	$ 83	$100
310	Food, Beverage, & Tobacco	31.1	15.6	14.7	9.4	7.4	10.6	$ 92	$131
321	Textiles	40.1	20.1	18.9	12.1	8.3	11.3	$ 461	$628
322	Wearing Apparel	73.7	36.9	34.8	22.3	18.0	11.7	$ 136	$ 89
323	Leather Products	15.2	7.6	7.2	4.6	3.3	0	$ 12	0
324	Footwear	33.7	16.9	15.9	10.2	10.2	2.2	$ 5	$ 1
331	Wood Products	11.6	5.8	5.5	3.5	2.2	0	$ 3	0
332	Furniture & Fixtures	27.5	13.8	13.0	8.3	4.9	0	$ 12	0
341	Paper & Paper Products	13.0	6.5	6.1	3.9	2.8	.6	$ 26	$ 6
342	Printing & Publishing	7.2	3.6	3.4	2.2	1.4	11.7	$ 6	$ 47
35A	Chemicals	25.1	12.6	11.9	7.6	5.1	.4	$ 569	$ 45
35B	Petroleum & Related Products	4.2	2.1	2.0	1.3	1.3	22.3	$ 9	$157
355	Rubber Products	14.6	7.3	6.9	4.4	3.1	0	$ 65	0
36A	Non-Metallic Mineral Products	23.6	11.8	11.1	7.1	4.7	.6	$ 89	$ 11
362	Glass & Glass Products	34.1	17.1	16.1	10.3	6.9	0	$ 45	0
371	Iron & Steel	18.2	9.1	8.6	5.5	4.2	15.2	$ 638	$2,307
372	Non-Ferrous Metals	6.4	3.2	3.0	1.9	1.5	0	$ 25	0
381	Metal Products	25.3	12.7	12.0	7.7	5.1	.2	$ 223	$ 9
382	Non-Electric Machinery	18.8	9.4	8.9	5.7	3.9	0	$1,233	0
383	Electric Machinery	27.5	13.8	13.0	8.3	6.2	5.8	$2,534	$2,370
384	Transport Equipment	22.6	11.3	10.6	6.8	5.2	9.4	$2,954	$5,340
38A	Misc. Manufacturing	25.9	13.0	12.2	7.8	5.0	1.1	$ 551	$ 121
Total Tariff Revenue[a]		$45,900	$22,950	$21,580	$13,860			$9,770	
Average Tariff Rate		24.1	12.1	11.3	7.3			5.1	
Total Tariff Equivalent Revenue									$11,362
Average Nontariff Barrier Tariff Equivalent									6.0

Sources: Baldwin (1984); Berthet-Bondet, Blades, and Pin (1988); Deardorff and Stern (1984); Saxonhouse and Stern (1989); and Sazanami (1989).

Note: All figures are ad valorem percentages.

[a] Using 1985 import levels in millions of 1988 dollars.

levels were each given 25 percent weight, as representative of the European Economic Community (EEC). Other countries were not included for simplicity and because detailed estimates of their tariff levels were not available. The assumption is that Japan faces the same tariffs imposed by these countries as any other exporter would face.

The harmful effects of tariffs, quotas, and VERs have been discussed. To try to understand how important these barriers are, we can look at the level of the tariffs facing Japanese goods. These are the taxes imposed by Japan's trading partners on goods imported from Japan. By applying these tax rates on goods actually exported from Japan, we obtain an estimate of the tax revenue collected by Japan's trading partners on Japanese exports. If Japan did not export much of a commodity, there will not be much tariff revenue associated with that commodity, even if it faces a high tariff.

The highest tariff levels facing Japan's exports are on wearing apparel (18.0%), footwear (10.2%), and textiles (8.3%). As can be seen in column G, the greatest tariff revenue occurs from transport equipment ($2.9 billion), electric machinery ($2.5 billion), and nonelectric machinery ($1.2 billion). Other important levels of tariff revenue on Japan's exports occur from textiles ($461 million), chemicals ($569 million), iron and steel ($638 million), and miscellaneous manufacturing ($551 million).

Column G gives the approximate tariff revenue in each industrial category. It is derived by multiplying the tariff levels in column E by the value of Japan's exports in the appropriate categories. The exports are reported in yen values by ISIC in Berthet-Bondet, Blades, and Pin (1988). The yen values are translated to 1985 dollars at the annual average exchange rate of 239 yen per dollar. The 1985 dollar figures were then adjusted by the U.S. gross national product (GNP) deflator to convert the figures to 1988 dollars.

The average tariff level facing Japan's exports after the Tokyo Round of GATT negotiations is 5.1 percent. This is simply the sum of all the tariff revenue on Japan's exports divided by the value of Japan's exports. The tariff revenue, of course, accrues to Japan's trading partners that impose the tariffs.

The total tariff revenue and average tariff rate on Japan's exports for prior years were calculated as though the same amount and value of trade occurred in earlier years as in 1985. Also, I assumed that all tariffs were cut proportionally. The average tariff cuts were taken to be as reported by Baldwin (1984), based on Lavergne (1981). Such an approach is illustrative of how high tariff barriers used to be. For every dollar of tariffs collected for given levels of trade in 1930, only 21 cents would be collected in tariffs today on the same amount of trade. Of course, if tariffs were as high today as in 1930, we would not have as much international trade. Also, many of the products traded today did not even exist in 1930.

TARIFF EQUIVALENTS OF NONTARIFF BARRIERS FACING JAPAN

The tariff equivalents of formal nontariff barriers facing Japan's exports are presented in column F of table 4.1. As is the case with tariffs, a high tariff equivalent of a nontariff barrier indicates a restrictive barrier equivalent to a tax imposed on imports from Japan. Nontariff barriers do tend to be more discriminatory than tariffs. Japan has sometimes been the only country affected. If Japan does not export much of a good that is subject to nontariff barriers, the revenue equivalent will be low, even with a restrictive high tariff equivalent.

The highest tariff equivalents are on Japan's exports of petroleum and related products (22.3%), iron and steel (15.2%), wearing apparel (11.7%), and printing and publishing (11.7%). Of these categories, only iron and steel ($2.3 billion) has substantial tariff equivalent revenue. Other categories of Japanese exports that generate large tariff equivalent revenue are transport equipment ($5.3 billion), electric machinery ($2.4 billion), and textiles ($628 million). The total level of tariff equivalent revenue on Japan's exports is $11.4 billion. The average tariff equivalent on all of Japan's exports from nontariff barriers is 6.0 percent. Since a number of the nontariff barriers are the result of voluntary export restraints, the tariff equivalent revenue will be partly captured by Japan in higher export prices. Some of it may also be captured by importers and distributors in the various countries importing from Japan.

Column F is a weighted average of the nontariff barrier equivalents of the United States (.5), France (.25), and Germany (.25), as reported in Saxonhouse and Stern (1989, table 9.4) and adapted from Deardorff and Stern (1987). The United States and countries in the EEC discriminate against Japan's exports of cars and consumer electronics with voluntary export restraints (Shepherd, 1982). Consequently, in estimating the level of barriers against Japan, I doubled the level of tariff equivalents for electric machinery and transport equipment. Since the equivalents reported by Saxonhouse and Stern are weighted by imports, the average for all imports in the category will be lower than the equivalents for Japan.

Table 4.2 presents estimates of nontariff barriers facing Japanese exports at various points in time for selected categories. Column D presents some of the estimates from columns F and H of table 4.1, based on Saxonhouse and Stern. These estimates are for the level of nontariff barriers in the 1970s and 1980s. Turner (1981, 1983) found the level of tariff equivalents of quantitative restrictions to vary considerably from year to year. His estimates of tariff equivalents covered the period from 1962 to 1977. Column B reports the lowest estimates of tariff equivalents of Japan's VERs on goods shipped to the United States. Column C reports the

Table 4.2
Nontariff Barriers to Japanese Exports

	Roningen & Yeats 1973 (A)[a]	Turner's Estimates in 1960s & 1970s Low (B)[b]	High (C)[b]	Saxonhouse & Stern 1970s & 1980s (D)[c]
Textiles				
Tariff Equivalents	37.5	3.7	47.6	11.3
Tariff Equivalent Revenue[d]	$2,084.0	$206.0	$2,645.0	$628.0
Wearing Apparel				
Tariff Equivalents	37.5	6.2	49.5	11.7
Tariff Equivalent Revenue[d]	$285.0	$47.0	$377.0	$89.0
Iron & Steel				
Tariff Equivalents	NA	8.4	21.6	15.2
Tariff Equivalent Revenue[d]	NA	$1,275.0	$3,278.0	$2,307.0
Electrical Machinery				
Tariff Equivalents	NA	NA	NA	5.8
Tariff Equivalent Revenue[d]	NA	NA	NA	$2,370.0
Transport Equipment				
Tariff Equivalents	NA	NA	NA	9.4
Tariff Equivalent Revenue[d]	NA	NA	NA	$5,340.0

Sources: Berthet-Bondet, Blades, and Pin (1988); Roningen and Yeats (1976); Saxonhouse and Stern (1989); and Turner (1981).

[a] Tariff equivalents are the average reported for the United States and France in Roningen and Yeats (1976, p. 620).

[b] Turner's estimates are U.S. tariff equivalents on Japan's exports, with highest and lowest estimates provided.

[c] Tariff equivalents are the weighted average of barriers for the United States, France, and Germany, as reported in Saxonhouse and Stern (1989, Table 9.4). The levels for electrical machinery and transport equipment were doubled.

[d] Tariff equivalent revenues are calculated using 1985 import values reported in Berthet-Bondet, Blades, and Pin (1988) in millions of 1988 dollars.

highest level of tariff equivalents for such restraints. Roningen and Yeats (1976) used price differences of selected goods to estimate tariff equivalents of nontariff barriers. The tariff equivalents for textiles and wearing apparel reported here are the average of the tariff equivalents on apparel for France and the United States. European countries have maintained residual quantitative restrictions against Japan on a bilateral basis throughout the postwar period (Meynell, 1982, pp. 113–16). These restrictions are almost surely underestimated using the present approach. Tariff equivalent revenues are reported for the different tariff equivalents using the level of Japan's exports in 1985 adjusted to 1988 prices.

In examining nontariff barriers, one is struck with what a confusing array of information is necessary to even estimate the impact of a quota or voluntary export restraint. As Staiger, Deardorff, and Stern say, "Unfortunately, since we lack methodologically consistent, accurate, and up to date information, we have no way of knowing what in fact the correct ad valorem equivalents should be" (1987, p. 169). It is quite likely that the difficulty in estimating the effects of nontariff barriers is part of their appeal to the various interest groups that lobby for their adoption.

Tariffs are more obvious than quotas and voluntary export restraints in their effects. As a consequence, it may be harder to get agreement to impose a very high tariff on imports when an export restraint of similar effect might be allowed. For instance, U.S. consumers did not get up in arms when the United States forced Japan to enter into a VER on automobiles. The argument was that these restraints would save American jobs in the automobile industry. Tarr and Morkre estimate that U.S. consumers suffered extra annual costs of $251,600 in 1984 dollars for each job that was protected by the restraint agreement (1987, p. 221). Opponents of such protectionist measures would have had heavy ammunition against any legislation of a tariff high enough to have cost so much. With quotas and VERs, it is only later that economists can decipher what the approximate effects are. Even the workers involved might find it hard to justify a cost of more than a quarter of a million dollars a year to consumers for every job in the auto industry that was saved.

SUMMARY

Japanese exports have faced many trade barriers in other countries. Some of these barriers, such as tariffs, have been common to any country trying to export goods to particular countries, except for various preferential agreements among countries like the EEC. Even these preferential agreements treat most outsiders in the same way. Most of these tariff levels have been successfully reduced by a series of multilateral trade negotiations. Japan's exports face lower hurdles as a result.

Quantitative restrictions and other nontariff barriers to Japanese exports have not been uniformly reduced. Throughout the postwar period, Japan has been singled out as a target for discriminatory application of various nontariff barriers. It seems clear that part of the reason for such discrimination is the remarkable success of Japan in achieving rapid economic growth. Japan's increase in exports of numerous goods has tended to cause dislocation in various industries among its trading partners. Restrictive measures have often followed. The level of these nontariff barriers changes from year to year. Generally, the protection provided is greater than that still provided by tariffs. Often, consumers in the countries imposing restrictions pay dearly for protection of domestic jobs in some specific industry threatened with Japanese competition.

5 Trade Barriers to Japanese Imports

Japan has participated in the general reduction in tariff barriers in the postwar period. The Japanese system of import administration has evolved from a quota system where approval had to be granted for virtually all types of imports (International Monetary Fund, 1956) to a system of relatively free trade. Over a period of years, numerous commodities were liberalized and moved to the automatic approval list. Items on the automatic approval list could be imported as long as foreign exchange was available (Ho, 1973). At present, there are few items remaining on a residual negative list requiring specific quota approval. Rice, citrus, and beef remain restricted. Most remaining official nontariff barriers are applied to food and agricultural items.

Rice, citrus, and beef imports have been subject to intense discussions between Japan and the United States. For a number of years, the quotas on citrus and beef have been substantially increased and are thus less restrictive. On the other hand, imports of rice are still substantially prohibited.

RICE

The prohibition on rice imports is undoubtedly the most important to Japan's economy. An analysis of its effect shows how distortional a quota can be. It also demonstrates that most of the damage from restricting a widely available commodity like rice falls on the country imposing the quota.

It has been estimated that the tariff equivalent of the rice import prohibition is about 700 percent (*The Wall Street Journal,* June 18, 1990, p. A8). Such a high tariff would cause very little rice to be imported, just as the prohibition does presently. The indication, then, is that the Japanese pay about eight times as much for rice as they would have to if it were freely importable.

In 1985, Japan produced and consumed about 15 million metric tons of rice. This and other data about rice production, trade, and pricing comes from the U.S. Department of Agriculture, *Agricultural Statistics.* The United States is the second-largest rice-exporting country. The price of rice in the United States in 1985 was about $175 per metric ton. Japanese rice consumption was worth about $2.6 billion at the U.S. price. The Japanese currently pay about $21 billion for this amount of rice. So, if the world price of rice stayed the same and Japan's rice import restrictions were lifted, the world's exports to Japan would increase by about $2.6 billion. Japanese consumers would save $18.4 billion. It is reasonably clear from these rough calculations that the barrier is more important for internal Japanese distributional reasons than it is to Japan's trading partners. Nevertheless, there are a number of issues related to protectionism that are illustrated by the rice barrier, so I will carry the analysis further.

If Japan were to eliminate the rice quota, the new world equilibrium price would probably be higher than at present. In judging which countries obtain the benefits of trade, a simple rule of thumb is that countries gain in proportion to the difference between the price of the good before trade and after trade. Thus, to find out how much rice-exporting countries might gain, we would like to know how much the world price might rise if trade in rice were freed.

The first thing that would likely happen with Japanese liberalization is that the price of rice would rise sharply. This is because world exports of rice in 1985 were only 12 million metric tons. If Japan imported 15 million metric tons, world exports would more than double. Much of the rice produced in the world, however, is produced for domestic consumption in countries such as China and India that do not have free and open trading economies. Given time, it seems likely that foreign supply of rice exports is fairly elastic. That is, a small rise in price that is expected to persist would result in a substantial increase in rice exports.

If Japan's production and consumption of rice is compared to worldwide production of rice, it is only 3 percent. If Japan stopped producing rice altogether, the rest of the world would only have to increase rice production by 3.3 percent to provide the same amount of rice.

If all of Japan's rice were to be provided by the United States, things would be more disruptive. The United States only produces 42 percent as much rice as Japan. So to provide Japan's rice, its own rice, and the 3.0

percent of its present rice production that it exports, the United States would have to produce 3.4 times as much rice as it does currently. Of course, the United States would not provide all of Japan's rice, so this is an extreme scenario. Nevertheless, allocating the necessary 3.4 times the present number of acres to produce 3.4 times as much rice, the United States would only be using 13 percent of the acres presently used to produce wheat. Further, rice and wheat together are only about 21 percent of total grain production in the United States. So, even if the United States had to supply all of the extra rice, if the change were affected over a long period of time, it is unlikely that the price of rice would have to rise substantially.

The demonstration that agricultural exporters could supply the extra rice without much of an increase in price indicates that their gains from the extra trade will be modest. Of course, it is likely that the Japanese will consume more rice if its price is lower. This might provide more of a challenge to the world supply system, but would be unlikely to change the basic results outlined above.

The higher relative price of rice, together with other changes in dietary patterns, has led to a decline in the amount of rice produced and consumed in Japan. From 1975 to 1985, rice production fell 13 percent. Land in rice production fell 15 percent over the same period. World production of rice increased by 34 percent over this same ten-year period. A rough guesstimate that Japan might consume 33 percent more rice if it were available at world prices shows lost consumer surplus from this cause to be $3 billion. This comes from the calculation of the area of a triangle with the extra quantity of rice as the base (.33 × 15 million metric tons), and the increased price due to quotas as the height (700 percent × $175 per metric ton). This calculation assumes the world price of rice would be the same if Japan liberalized imports. While $3 billion is not large as a percentage of Japan's gross national product (GNP), it is larger than the total increase in exports of rice from Japan's liberalization. It is another indication that Japan's rice prohibition is primarily hurting Japanese consumers rather than foreign suppliers. Of course, this is one reason foreign governments have not been more insistent on Japan's liberalization in this area.

The high price of rice and other agricultural products also distorts the production process. Staiger, Deardorff, and Stern (1987, p. 178) conclude that Japanese agriculture employment would be substantially reduced if Japan removed all tariffs and nontariff barriers. As agricultural production in Japan fell, so too would the rents paid to agricultural landholders. According to the Stolper-Samuelson theorem (1941) and in a specific factors model (Caves, Frankel, and Jones, 1990, pp. 112–14), the rents on land would fall more in percentage terms than the commodity prices. Since full rice liberalization would cause rice prices to fall 87 percent, land prices for rice production would need to fall more than this for rice production to remain possible. Since land in Japan is scarce and has many alternative uses, the probable result is that virtually all rice farming would cease.

At the present time, the value of land in farming in Japan is putting a high floor price on land in Japan. The value of land in Japan is more than four times the value of all land in the United States, even though Japan has only 4 percent of the land area of the United States (Hayashi, 1989; Moffat, 1990, p. 113). Eliminating agricultural import barriers would need to be done carefully to avoid a sudden collapse in real estate values in Japan.

How can trade restrictions on $2.6 billion worth of rice (at U.S. prices) have much effect on the value of Japanese land? The answers are illuminating for general equilibrium effects and investment markets. To make our task simpler, we will approach the answer in a time-honored approach for economists. We will make a number of assumptions so that we can avoid many complications and focus on the basic process of valuation of the land. Assumptions:

1. With free trade, 50 percent of the value of output goes to land rents.
2. Rice would continue to be produced with and without the quota.
3. Nonland input costs of rice production do not rise with higher tariff equivalents.
4. The discount rate for agricultural land rents in Japan is 2 percent.
5. People tend to project past trends forward.

With the above assumptions, we can calculate the value of rice-producing land with free trade. If all land presently yielding rice were used with free trade, $2.6 billion of rice would be produced. This would provide $1.3 billion of land rent, using the 50 percent land rent (assumption 1). Given a 2 percent discount rate (assumption 4), the price of rice-producing lands would be $65 billion, with the belief that prices would remain constant. This is the present value of $1.3 billion per year in perpetuity at a 2 percent discount rate.

If Japan moved from free trade to the present level of protection, rice sales by farmers would be $21 billion. If landowners captured all of the increase in revenue (assumption 3), land rents would be $19.7 billion. Land values for rice-producing farms would rise to $985 billion at a 2 percent discount rate (assumption 4), on the assumption of constant future prices. Given the tendency to project past trends (assumption 5), the

Japanese are likely to project rapid appreciation of land prices into the future. After all, on the basis of these simple calculations, land prices went up more than fifteen times. If the Japanese expected another fifteen times increase, they would be looking at expected land valuation of $15 trillion.

The above is meant to be suggestive of the direction and magnitude of the effects of Japan's trade barriers. It is not a detailed or rigorous analysis. Still, it sheds light on why the Japanese pay so much for housing that seems inadequate given their high income levels. Changes in Japan's trade barriers are directly linked to changes in land use and housing affordability.

JAPANESE TARIFFS

Japanese tariff rates have been cut successively as part of the multilateral General Agreement on Tariffs and Trade (GATT) talks. In addition, Japan has recently cut rates when other countries have not, to further open access to Japanese markets. This has been done in part to try to reduce the Japanese trade surplus. The levels of tariff and nontariff barriers are still important in showing the industries that Japan is trying to protect. The magnitudes are lower now than in the past; nevertheless, these tariffs represent billions of dollars of import tax revenue or quasi-taxes collected by beneficiaries of importing and exporting privileges. The actual levels of these barriers are thus important to an understanding of Japanese trade policy.

Japanese tariff and nontariff barriers to imports are reported in table 5.1. The same basic approach is used as in table 4.1, which showed the barriers to Japanese exports. Column E reports average tariff levels by industry, as reported by Saxonhouse and Stern (1989). These averages are derived by using Japanese imports as weights. The three Japanese industries with the highest tariff levels in the Saxonhouse and Stern study are food, beverages and tobacco (28.5%), agriculture, forestry, and fisheries (21.8%), and footwear (15.7%). The three Japanese industries with the lowest tariff levels are printing and publishing (.1%), wood products (.3%), and nonmetallic mineral products (.5%).

Column G reflects the reduction in tariffs from the level reported in Saxonhouse and Stern as a result of the Japanese Action Program for the Improvement of Market Access (Sazanami, 1989, p. 100). The detail level is developed under the presumption that the 1986 cuts were evenly distributed over the industry categories. These tariff levels were then used to calculate the tariff revenues by industry that are reported in column H. The 1985 Japanese import values by industry reported in Berthet-

Table 5.1
Tariffs and Tariff Equivalents of Other Trade Barriers to Japanese Imports

ISIC	Industry Category	1930 Tariffs (A)	1955 Tariffs (B)	Pre-Kennedy Round (C)	Pre-Tokyo Round (D)	Post-Tokyo Round Tariffs (E)	Post-Tokyo Round NTB (F)	After 1986 Tariffs (G)	Tariff Revenue[b] (H)	Tariff Equiv. Revenue[b] (I)
1--	Agriculture, Forestry, & Fisheries	72.1	36.1	34.1	21.8[a]	21.8	48.5	16.8	$4,925	$14,217
310	Food, Beverage, & Tobacco	94.2	47.2	44.5	28.5[a]	28.5	27.1	21.9	$1,650	$ 2,041
321	Textiles	11.0	5.5	5.2	3.3[a]	3.3	5.2	2.5	$ 70	$ 146
322	Wearing Apparel	45.9	23.0	21.7	13.9[a]	13.9	2.7	10.7	$ 255	$ 64
323	Leather Products	10.2	5.1	4.8	3.1[a]	3.1	0	2.4	$ 8	0
324	Footwear	54.1	27.1	25.6	16.4	15.7	6.1	12.1	$ 38	$ 19
331	Wood Products	1.0	.5	.5	.3	.3	0	.2	$ 4	0
332	Furniture & Fixtures	25.7	12.9	12.2	7.8	5.1	0	3.9	$ 12	0
341	Paper & Paper Products	9.6	4.8	4.5	2.9[a]	2.9	0	2.2	$ 35	0
342	Printing & Publishing	.6	.3	.3	.2	.1	0	.1	0	0
35A	Chemicals	20.6	10.3	9.7	6.2	4.8	1.1	3.7	$ 448	$ 103
35B	Petroleum & Related Products	9.4	4.7	4.4	2.8	2.2	1.3	1.7	$1,341	$ 792
355	Rubber Products	4.8	2.4	2.3	1.5	1.1	0	.8	$ 2	0
36A	Non-Metallic Mineral Products	2.0	1.0	.9	.6	.5	1.1	.4	$ 2	$ 5
362	Glass & Glass Products	24.8	12.4	11.7	7.5	5.1	0	3.9	$ 9	0
371	Iron & Steel	11.0	5.5	5.2	3.3	2.8	0	2.2	$ 37	0
372	Non-Ferrous Metals	3.6	1.8	1.7	1.1	1.1	0	.8	$ 38	0
381	Metal Products	22.8	11.4	10.8	6.9	5.2	0	4.0	$ 27	0
382	Non-Electric Machinery	30.1	15.1	14.2	9.1	4.4	0	3.4	$ 151	0
383	Electric Machinery	24.6	12.3	11.6	7.4	4.3	0	3.3	$ 125	0
384	Transport Equipment	20.0	10.0	9.4	6.0	1.5	0	1.2	$ 76	0
38A	Misc. Manufacturing	20.0	10.0	9.4	6.0	4.6	.8	3.5	$ 157	$ 36
Total Tariff Revenue[c]		$57.0	$28.6	$27.1	$17.3	$12.2	$17.4	$9.4	$9.4	
Average Tariff Rate									6.6	
Total Tariff Equivalent Revenue										$17.4
Average Nontariff Barrier Tariff Equivalent										12.3

Sources: Baldwin (1984); Berthet-Bondet, Blades, and Pin (1988); Deardorff and Stern (1984); Saxonhouse and Stern (1989); and Sazanami (1989).

[a] Figures for Saxonhouse and Stern were used where Deardorff and Stern indicated no change in tariff levels.
[b] Using 1985 import levels in millions of 1988 dollars.
[c] Using 1985 import levels in billions of 1988 dollars.

Bondet, Blades, and Pin (1988) are adjusted to 1985 current dollars at 239 yen per dollar. The 1985 dollars are then converted to 1988 dollars using the GNP price deflator.

Estimated 1985 Japanese tariff revenue by industry is reported in column H in 1988 dollars. The industries with the highest tariff revenues are agriculture, forestry, and fisheries ($4.9 billion), food, beverages, and tobacco ($1.7 billion), and petroleum and related products ($1.3 billion). The industries with the lowest tariff revenue are printing and publishing (less than $1 million), nonmetallic mineral products ($2 million), and rubber products ($2 million). The food industry had higher average tariffs, but agriculture had a higher level of imports, which accounts for the switch in these two measures of import protection. The only reason petroleum and related products made the list of major protected items in terms of revenue is because fuels accounted for over $60 billion of Japan's imports in 1985.

Column D of table 5.1 shows the level of tariffs prior to the Tokyo Round of GATT negotiations, weighted by Japan's imports, as reported in Deardorff and Stern (1984), except for those industries with no change in tariff levels. These have been assigned the later figures in Saxonhouse and Stern (1989). The relative positioning of the most-protected and least-protected industries stayed the same as in column E. Columns A, B, and C show detailed industry tariffs on a pro rata basis. The simplifying assumptions are that the tariff levels were equally reduced in the various GATT negotiating rounds and that the weighting by imports stayed the same. Since these assumptions are counter-factual, the industry level of tariffs in earlier periods is merely illustrative of orders of magnitude of these barriers.

The approximate level of Japanese tariff revenue in 1985 would have been $9.4 billion in 1988 dollars if the post-1986 tariff levels had been in place. With the weighting used by Deardorff and Stern (1986), which was 1976 Japanese imports, tariff revenue in Japan in 1985 would have been $12.2 billion, in 1988 dollars.

Using the same weightings and import levels as in column E, the total tariff revenue level that would have occurred with the higher tariff rates in earlier periods can be calculated. The pre-Tokyo Round level would have been $17.3 billion in 1988 dollars. The pre-Kennedy Round level of tariff revenue would have been $27.1 billion in 1988 dollars. The 1955 tariff revenue level would have been $28.6 billion, and the 1930 tariff revenue level under these assumptions would have been $57.0 billion in 1988 dollars. The purpose of this exercise is to give an idea of the magnitude of earlier tariff barriers in Japan compared to the present. Consumer welfare would be considerably lower now, as would Japanese imports, if tariffs had not been decreased. The loss to consumers probably would have been at least several times the amount of the tariff revenue.

JAPANESE NONTARIFF BARRIERS

Formal Japanese nontariff barriers are now more than twice as restrictive as tariff barriers. In the immediate postwar period, virtually all Japanese imports were subject to quotas and administrative control. Importers had to obtain permission to import particular goods, and then could seek the foreign exchange necessary to complete the import transaction. During the 1960s more than 2,000 commodity categories were liberalized so that special permission was no longer required (Turner, 1989, p. 84).

Column F in table 5.1 shows estimates of tariff equivalents of Japanese nontariff barriers estimated by Deardorff and Stern (1987) and reported by Saxonhouse and Stern (1989). These tariff equivalents by industry are weighted by Japanese imports, just as the tariff levels were. Of course, this means that almost no weight is given to the extremely restrictive barrier to rice imports that was explored earlier in this chapter. In spite of attaching almost no weight to rice barriers, the nontariff equivalent to imports of agriculture, forestry, and fisheries is extremely high, at 48.5 percent. This is almost three times as restrictive as the 16.8 percent tariff level on imports in this category. Together, the tariffs and nontariff barriers are equivalent to a tariff of 65.3 percent. Remember, too, this very restrictive level would be much higher if rice restrictions were entered with a weighting by consumption or production instead of imports.

The second most restrictive nontariff barriers are on imports of food, beverage, and tobacco products (27.1%). This is somewhat more restrictive than the 21.9 percent level of tariffs in this category (see table 5.1, columns F and G). Together, the tariffs and nontariff barriers are equivalent to a tariff of 49 percent. The next most restrictive nontariff barriers are on textiles (5.2%). Imports of silk products are the most restricted in the textile categories.

There are thirteen industrial categories where no formal nontariff barriers exist. This reflects the tremendous liberalization process that has gone on in Japan over the last three decades. As Japan has progressed into an economic and trading powerhouse, it has been under almost continual pressure to expand access to its markets. By and large, it has done so. Most remaining nontariff barriers are in food and agriculture.

When nontariff barriers are considered from the viewpoint of tariff revenue equivalents, the most restrictive barriers remain on agriculture, forestry, and fisheries ($14.2 billion in 1988 dollars). The second most restrictive are on food, beverage, and tobacco products ($2.0 billion in 1988 dollars). The third most restrictive Japanese nontariff barriers in terms of revenue are on petroleum and related products, rather than textiles. The tariff equivalent is only 1.3 percent, but since imports in this

Table 5.2
Nontariff Barriers to Selected Japanese Imports (Weighted by Imports)

	Roningen & Yeats (1973) (A)	Turner's Estimates 1960s & 1970s Low (B)	Turner's Estimates 1960s & 1970s High (C)	Saxonhouse & Stern 1970s & 1980s (D)
Agriculture, Forestry, & Fisheries				
Tariff Equivalents (percent)	70.0	12.2[a]	48.5[a]	48.5
Tariff Equivalent Revenue[b]	$20,519	$3,576	$14,217	$14,217
Food, Beverage & Tobacco				
Tariff Equivalents (percent)	90.0	12.2[a]	48.5[a]	27.1
Tariff Equivalent Revenue	$ 6,780	$ 919	$ 3,654	$ 2,041
Textiles				
Tariff Equivalents (percent)	NA	1.5	12.0	5.2
Tariff Equivalent Revenue[b]	NA	$ 42	$ 338	$ 146
Wearing Apparel				
Tariff Equivalents (percent)	5.0	NA	NA	2.7
Tariff Equivalent Revenue[b]	$ 119	NA	NA	$ 64
Leather Products				
Tariff Equivalents (percent)	NA	1.0	45.0	0
Tariff Equivalent Revenue[b]	NA	$ 3	$ 150	0
Footwear				
Tariff Equivalents (percent)	11.0	0	613.8	6.1
Tariff Equivalent Revenue[b]	$ 34	0	$ 1,909	$ 19
Petroleum & Related Products				
Tariff Equivalents (percent)	NA	0	17.9	1.3
Tariff Equivalent Revenue[b]	NA	0	$10,908	$ 792
Coal				
Tariff Equivalents (percent)	NA	0	78.4	0
Tariff Equivalent Revenue[b]	NA	0	$ 3,750	0

Agricultural Protection (percentage), Weighted by Production (includes tariff & nontariff barriers)[c]

	1955	1965	1975	1984	1986
Japan	18	69	76	102	210
EEC	35	45	29	22	63
US	2	9	4	6	6

Sources: Berthet-Bondet, Blades, and Pin (1988); Honma (1989); Roningen and Yeats (1976); Saxonhouse and Stern (1989); and Turner (1981).

[a] Combined into SITC 0.
[b] Tariff equivalent revenues are calculated using 1985 import levels in millions of 1988 dollars as reported in Berthet-Bondet, Blades, and Pin (1988).
[c] From Honma (1989).

category are over $60 billion, the tariff revenue equivalent is $792 million in 1988 dollars. Of course, the categories with zero tariff equivalents have zero tariff revenue equivalents.

Table 5.2 presents estimates of nontariff barriers facing Japanese imports in selected categories at various points in time. Estimates are provided from three different studies. Deardorff and Stern (1987) results as reported in table 5.1 are repeated in column D for the commodity categories examined here. Roningen and Yeats (1976) estimated tariff equivalents for some categories of Japanese imports in 1973. These results for agriculture, food, wearing apparel, and footwear are reported in column A. Turner (1981, 1989) reported various levels of tariff equivalents in commodity categories for the 1960s and 1970s. The high and low estimates by Turner (1981) are reported for various commodity categories in column C. The tariff equivalent revenue reported in table 5.2 is the product of the tariff equivalent for the category and the value of imports in the category in 1985, adjusted to 1988 dollars. Variations in the level of tariff equivalent revenue are thus useful in viewing changes in the restrictiveness of the nontariff levels.

For all of the commodity categories except agriculture, forestry, and fisheries, Japanese nontariff barriers are lower in the most recent period than they were in some previous period. The tariff equivalent of Japanese nontariff barriers on food, beverages, and tobacco was 90.0 percent in 1973, and is 27.1 percent now. In 1988 dollars, an extra $4.7 billion would have been generated in tariff-equivalent revenue in 1985 if the higher barriers had been in place. Since such tariff-equivalent revenue is only one part of the extra cost to consumers, Japanese consumers probably benefited by much more than $5 billion from the lowering of barriers on food. Textiles had barriers equivalent to 12 percent in 1963, versus 5.2 percent in 1985. Barriers on wearing apparel and footwear were once about twice as high as they were in 1985.

Nontariff barriers on leather products and coal have disappeared entirely. Prior levels of nontariff barriers on coal would have cost Japanese consumers more than $4 billion in 1985 if they had still been in place. As reported in chapter 3, coal imports increased from 6.4 percent of total consumption to 84.1 percent by 1985. This increase was to a large degree due to the lowering of Japanese nontariff barriers to coal imports. The Japanese economy has benefited by having coal available at lower prices. The United States and other coal-exporting countries have benefited by being able to export more coal at a higher price than would have prevailed without Japan's imports.

Agricultural nontariff barriers have strengthened over time instead of diminishing, in spite of several expansions of quotas. Roningen and Yeats show Japanese agricultural nontariff barriers to be 70 percent in 1973. Deardorff and Stern use 48.5 percent for agricultural barriers for the most recent period. This indicates a fall of 21.5 percent in tariff equivalents, or 31 percent of the level in 1973. However, this is more likely due to the difference in weighting than to a true difference in levels of nontariff barriers.

Agricultural protection in different years, including tariffs and nontariff barriers, was estimated by Honma and Hayami (1986) and Hayami and Honma (1987) for Japan, the European Economic Community (EEC), and the United States. They estimate tariff equivalents for Japan of 18 percent in 1955 and 210 percent in 1986. Their estimates are weighted on a production basis instead of an import basis. As already discussed, this would give additional weight to high barriers on commodities like rice, which have a high production level but few imports.

The drastic changes in tariff equivalents that can occur with market changes are also illustrated by the work of Honma and Hayami reported by Honma (1989). In 1984, Japan's agricultural protection level was 102 percent and the EEC's was 22 percent. In 1986, Japan's level was 210 percent and the EEC's was 63 percent. The major changes that occurred between 1984 and 1986 were the fall in the value of the dollar by 19 percent in terms of its trade-weighted average and the fall of 9 percent in farm product prices in dollar terms (U.S. President, 1990). The price fall would have been worse for Japanese farmers, since the dollar fell 39 percent against the yen from 1984 to 1986. To keep Japanese agricultural output at the same level with sharply lower international prices in yen, the tariff equivalents had to be much higher on agricultural commodities. This kept the Japanese consumer from benefiting from the low prices of agricultural commodities.

SUMMARY

Japan has participated in the various multilateral trade negotiations held under the auspices of GATT. Japan has lowered tariff barriers on manufactured and agricultural commodities in the postwar period. Most formal nontariff barriers in Japan have been removed. The tariff equivalents of the remaining Japanese nontariff barriers are lower than in the past, except on agricultural commodities. Tariff equivalents of agricultural barriers are extremely high, especially for rice.

Removal of the remaining agricultural nontariff barriers in Japan would help the United States and other agricultural exporters. The major effect, though, would be to benefit the Japanese consumer. Japanese land and agricultural workers would be reallocated to uses that would be more beneficial when evaluated at world prices. The extremely high valuation of land in Japan might well be reduced.

Japan does not seem to be atypical in its use of protectionist policies. It has used protection to shield declining industries, in part to cushion the effects of its changing comparative advantage (Honma, 1989, p. 169). Japan's extremely rapid growth has led to more attention being given to Japan regarding trade matters. Its high savings rate and global investment activities have led to higher trade surpluses, which have caused even greater negative scrutiny of its policies. We need to look into this area of essentially macroeconomic policy to understand why Japan has recently run persistently high balance of payments surpluses.

6 Macroeconomic Effects of Japan on the Global Economy

One country affects other countries in the global economy in four basic ways: (1) trading relationships, (2) investment flows, (3) technology transfer, and (4) migration. In the postwar period, migration to or from Japan has played only a minor role, so my discussion here will be limited to the other three mechanisms by which one country affects others.

We have already seen how trading relationships can make both trading groups better off. In the long run, with full employment and balance of trade equilibrium, welfare is improved by trading with other countries. The more one country differs from the rest of the world, the more it will benefit from trade, and the greater is the possible benefit to the rest of the world. Since Japan's resources and factors of production are quite different from those of the rest of the world, Japan has had a high degree of welfare improvement possible from trading with others.

Macroeconomics analyzes some of the short and intermediate problems of economics. We want to know what happens in trading relationships when an economy is not necessarily at full employment or balance of trade equilibrium. In this area, the effect a country has on its fellow countries is largely determined by how much it imports and exports.

As Japan has grown so dramatically over the postwar period, its imports and exports have grown even faster. In 1985, Japan's gross national product was 12 percent of the total GNP of the market economies. In 1955, Japan's gross national product (GNP) was only 3 percent of the GNP of the market economies. As a consequence, a change in Japan's growth rate or other macroeconomic characteristics would have more than four times the relative impact today than it had thirty years ago. The larger Japan becomes relative to the rest of the world, the more other economies are impacted by Japan's economic policies.

Japan has also become increasingly important with respect to investment flows. This is because Japan's pool of investable funds that can be used for foreign investments is larger relative to other countries than it was in the past. There are also more potential investments in Japan. Perhaps even more, though, it is because Japan now permits greater investments overseas by its citizens and domestic financial institutions and permits more inward-bound investments by foreign nationals.

Japan has also become a leader in technology. It transfers this technology in a number of ways. It sells advanced manufacturing equipment to others; it sells technologically advanced consumer goods; and it manufactures overseas using its own technology and management processes. Indications are that Japan's contributions to technological growth will continue to be extremely important in the global economy.

Japan's effects on the rest of the global economy are many and varied. The mechanisms by which changes in policies or underlying conditions are transmitted from Japan to its global trading partners are complicated, and are only partially captured in even the most elaborate global economic models used today. Rather than trying to fully specify an elaborate model or reviewing existing models, I will explore Japan's role by looking at several scenarios that depict events that have happened or that might happen. By looking at effects in the long run and the short and intermediate run, we can see how future developments might be affected by policy choices made in Japan. I will look at three specific scenarios: (1) slowing economic growth in Japan, (2) a reduction of protectionism in Japan, and (3) an increase in the relative preference of the Japanese for foreign investments.

SLOWING ECONOMIC GROWTH IN JAPAN

Since Japan is still growing faster than the United States and many countries in the European Economic Community (EEC), people frequently miss the fact that Japan's rate of growth is much lower over the recent period than it was in the earlier postwar period. Real GNP growth for Japan was 4.3 percent from 1974 to 1985. This was less than the rate for the twenty earlier years, although it was still faster than any other advanced industrial country (Lincoln, 1988, p. 39). What are the likely consequences of such a slowing of Japan's economy?

The first look at the effect of a slowing in the growth of an economy can be undertaken in the context of a closed system. Suppose Japan were an isolated economy. What would a lower rate of growth mean? The answer can provide insight into the types of stresses we can expect to see between Japan and other countries as a consequence of Japan's slower growth.

A country's growth rate can be considered a function of the rate of growth of its workforce, the rate of capital accumulation, the rate of technological change, the improvement in education (rate of increase in human capital), and the improvement in capital (Jorgenson, 1988). Referring back to table 1.1, we see that the Japanese workforce increased from 40 million in 1955 to 49 million in 1965. This is an increase of 22.5 percent for the ten year period. The Japanese workforce increased by 10.2 percent in the next decade, to 54 million in 1975. The increase was 11.1 percent in the next decade, to 60 million in 1985. The Japanese workforce is expected to increase only 5 percent in the current decade, to be 63 million in 1995. Clearly, the difference in the rate of growth in the Japanese economy between the decades ending in 1975 and 1985 cannot be attributed to a slower growth in the labor force. This is not surprising, though, since most of Japan's real economic growth has been real growth in per capita income. Japan's economic growth rate has far exceeded its population growth rate.

Capital accumulation in Japan has far exceeded the growth in population. Capital plant and equipment per worker was 380 percent of the 1955 level in 1965. In 1975, it was 391 percent of what it was in 1965, and it was 117 percent of the 1975 level in 1985. The dramatic slowdown from 1975 to 1985 in the rate of increase in capital per worker is what economic theory would predict.

As more of any factor of production is added to existing factors, its marginal product declines. That is, the extra output that can be attributed to the use of one more unit of capital will begin to decline at some point in the production process. This is observed frequently enough that it is called "the law of diminishing returns" (Lipsey and Steiner, 1981, pp. 190–92).

An economy tends to achieve a steady and sustainable rate of growth when the return to an extra unit of capital is just sufficient to cause it to be accumulated (Solow, 1970). Capital is accumulated by foregoing consumption in the current period so as to use resources in building capital equipment. There is some ambiguity as to the response of savings to the rate of return on savings; generally, economists expect savings to increase with increases in the real return to savings (Boskin, 1978; Summers, 1987). Equilibrium in the system occurs where the amount of capital per worker causes the return on capital to decline to the point that there is no further incentive to accumulate more capital by giving up additional consumption in the current period.

In the case of Japan in the postwar period, the capital stock per worker was increasing rapidly. Returns on the capital investment were very high, and the Japanese personal savings rate was the highest in the industrial world (Lincoln, 1988, p. 77). This was a major contributor to Japanese economic growth from 1955 to 1975. By 1975, Japan's capital per worker had caught up to that in the United States and West Germany (see table 1.1). Additional investment per worker would cause the return on capital to decline. The investment rate in Japan fell as a consequence. Nevertheless, the amount of capital per worker continued to grow and return on capital in Japan fell.

In a closed system, the eventual result of these forces would be for the return on capital and real interest rates to fall low enough that savings fall, until capital growth is just sufficient to provide new workers with a dollop of capital and replace the capital used up in the production process. In the process, there would be macroeconomic pressures that would affect employment and inflation. In an open system, there are complications brought about by trade balances, capital flows, and exchange rate changes.

Macroeconomic Effects of Slower Growth in Japan

The macroeconomy is in equilibrium when total planned spending in the economy is equal in magnitude to total output. All the producers can sell their products. This basically confirms the output decisions that were made. The result is that production processes continue pretty much on track. No major adjustments to prices or output are necessary.

When the level of investment falls, the tendency is for production to exceed aggregate demand. One remedy for this is for the government to increase its expenditures so that total expenditures stay at the expected level of output. Another alternative is to have an increase in consumption that keeps expenditure at the expected level. If neither of these adjustments occurs immediately, then output exceeds expenditures, and firms find themselves with unwanted inventory.

The unwanted inventory can be eliminated by an individual firm by cutting prices. However, if all firms cut prices at once, this is much less effective. Partly for this reason, many firms adjust output instead of, or perhaps in addition to, cutting prices. In Japan, when large firms lower output, they try to avoid layoffs. Smaller firms may have to lay off workers during a period when excess inventory is being sold off. Inventory is reduced by lowering output below the firm's rate of sales. Unfortunately, the decline in income associated with reduced output causes a reduction in consumption as well as a reduction in savings. Consequently, income has to fall much further than the original drop in investment before aggregate expenditure and output are equal again. This is the simple Keynesian multiplier effect. If, because of the uncertainties related to a slowing economy, people increase their savings rate, then the potential economic contraction is even more severe.

Usually, at some point in this adjustment process, the government would recognize the contraction that was taking place and would seek to remedy the situation. The Keynesian prescription for an economy in recession is some combination of stimulative fiscal policy and easy money policy. Fiscal policy is stimulative when government spending is increased or when taxes are decreased. An easy money policy would be to increase the money supply and thereby decrease short-term interest rates.

If government spending is increased, in the short run the effect on aggregate spending is the same as an increase in investment. On its face, this seems like a good remedy for a decrease in investments. It worked well in Japan as long as the fall in investment was temporary. Such decreases were quickly detected, and government spending was temporarily increased to offset the contraction until investment spending rose again. Listing such caveats shows where some problems associated with increasing government spending will likely arise. By and large, though, the Japanese have been better at keeping their economy at or near full employment than the United States and European countries have.

If the fall in investment levels is permanent or at least long lasting, then the substitution of government spending for private investment can have profound negative consequences. The major purpose of investment is not for the immediate results on employment, but for the provision of additional productive capacity in the future. Government spending on non-investment goods and services is an alternative to current consumption.

Normally, through some sort of decision-making process (democratic, bureaucratic, or autocratic), society determines how much of current goods and services should be provided privately and how much publicly. If this process is efficient, then an extra dollar spent by the government provides the same extra social welfare as an extra dollar spent on private consumption. If government spending is permanently increased to offset a reduction in investment, then the additional government projects undertaken will tend to be those that were judged to be "not worth it" in normal times. In other words, social resources could be used on projects that are not justified on their merits.

Reducing taxes, rather than raising government spending, tends to avoid the wasteful aspect of allocating too much of the economy's resources to public purposes. There are a few other problems with tax cuts, though. Tax cuts do not have as large a multiplier effect. This is partly because some of the taxes that no longer have to be paid are simply saved. Therefore, tax cuts would need to be larger than corresponding increases in government spending. Further, the speed of the counter-recessionary effect may be slower with taxes than a change in government spending.

There are also some problems with increasing the money supply to offset the contractional effects of reduced investment. The direct effect of an increased money supply will be a lower interest rate. This will act to stimulate investment, since there will be a lower real interest rate. The extra money will cause people to increase total spending, as they have a higher money balance than desired. This will lead to higher prices than would have occurred without the increase in the money supply.

As with so many economic changes, there are many different combinations of results that can take place. No one path of adjustment is guaranteed to take place. Policymakers have a major role to play in how the economy responds. Consumers and business leaders also make decisions that affect the ultimate outcome. The basic outcomes of reduced investment in a closed economy will be lower economic growth, greater consumption and government spending out of current income, lower interest rates, and perhaps, higher levels of inflation.

Repercussions on Trade and International Investment Flows from Slower Growth in Japan

Japan is part of the global trading and financial markets, and is not limited to the outcome for a closed economy. When reduced investment lowers effective demand for Japanese goods by domestic producers and consumers, Japanese firms can lower prices and sell more to foreigners. Japanese savers can invest in foreign countries, either directly or through financial intermediaries. As a consequence, the Japanese savings rate would not have to decline and government spending and taxes would not need to change as much as in a closed economy.

Under the condition that foreign countries simply continue their normal policies, we can look at the interaction effects of changes in Japan both in the long run and in the short run. In the first instance, when Japanese investment spending weakens, Japanese inventories start to build. If Japanese producers lower prices, foreigners will find Japanese goods more appealing and will import more. Japanese residents will also switch from buying foreign goods and will want to buy more Japanese goods because of their relatively lower price. Of course, buying more Japanese goods will only result in paying more for those goods if the percentage increase in goods sold is greater than the percentage fall in their price. In other words, if the elasticity of demand for Japanese goods is greater than 1.0, a fall in their price will lead to an increase in the value of their output. From an employment point of view, any increase in physical volume tends to sustain employment, but the foreign exchange market effects depend on elasticities.

Suppose the reduced prices of Japanese goods lead to a higher value of Japanese exports and a lower value of Japanese imports. At a given exchange rate (yen per dollar), there will be an increased demand for Japanese yen in the foreign exchange market and a reduction in the supply of the yen. If the Bank of Japan is trying to maintain the value of the yen, it will have to intervene in the foreign exchange market and supply yen (buy dollars). If the central bank sterilizes its foreign exchange market intervention, it would have to sell Japanese Treasury bills thereby keeping the Japanese money supply at the same level. If it does not sterilize such intervention with offsetting domestic monetary adjustments, the Japanese money supply will tend to increase and the foreign money supply will tend to decrease. The effect of such money supply changes will be to raise Japanese prices relative to foreign prices, and this effect will tend to offset the initial decrease in Japanese prices.

During the adjustment process, however, we need to remember the initiating cause of the disturbance. Japanese investment declined from the level expected, which was in line with the level of Japanese savings. Consequently, the amount being saved is potentially greater than the amount of domestic investment. If there were no foreign markets, the adjustment would be for real interest rates to fall. This would probably cause savings to diminish, and investments would almost surely increase. With foreign markets, the return on Japanese financial investments should be such that a market participant is indifferent between an extra 1,000 yen invested in Japan or the United States, Germany, or any other foreign country.

The possibility of foreign investment profoundly changes the expected effects of a disturbance in Japanese investment levels on the foreign exchange market. As the possibility of greater investment in Japanese plant and equipment decreases at the going rate of return on capital, the rate of return acceptable on Japanese investment will tend to fall. This, in turn, will make foreign financial investments, at the going rates, seem more appealing to Japanese financial investors. As a result, there would likely be an increase in the net demand for foreign assets by the Japanese. This increase in net demand for foreign assets could be greater or less than the increase in net exports caused by the fall in relative prices of Japanese goods.

The relative magnitudes of the change in net demand for foreign assets and the change in net exports determine the direction of changes in the foreign exchange market. If the change in net demand for foreign assets is greater than the change in net exports, then the combined effect is to increase the net demand for foreign currency. If the Bank of Japan were to defend a fixed exchange rate, it would have to intervene and sell dollars for yen. This would tend to increase the foreign money supply and reduce the Japanese money supply. The price effects would then further increase the relative price of foreign goods. This would strengthen the tendency for an increase in Japanese net exports. If the change in net demand for foreign assets is less than the change in net exports, the process of intervention will be similar to that discussed earlier. The intervention will tend to offset the initial decrease in Japanese prices, but the offset will not be complete. Private capital outflows from Japan tend to promote and confirm increases in Japan's net exports.

Matters are further complicated by changes in exchange rates. If Japan does not fix exchange rates, then whenever there is an increase in net demand for the yen, the value of the yen will increase (the yen/dollar exchange rate will fall). This means that if the increase in net demand for foreign assets is not as great as the increase in net exports, the value of the yen increases or the exchange rate falls. When the yen increases in value, it has the same allocational effect as a tax on exports and a subsidy to imports (Caves, Frankel, and Jones, 1990, p. 408). This, then, would tend to offset the initial fall in the relative prices of Japanese goods. Without capital flows, general uniform price changes in one country would just result in changes in exchange rates, with no real economic effects.

In a flexible exchange rate regime, if the increase in net demand for foreign assets is greater than the increase in net exports, the value of the yen will tend to fall. This will have the effect of further increasing the quantity of exports and reducing the quantity of imports. Under reasonable elasticity assumptions, eventually, after what is called the J-curve period of adjustment, the value of net exports will increase due to a devaluation of the yen. This will be a reinforcement of the original tendency for greater net exports caused by the lower relative price of Japanese goods.

The end results of these alternative paths of adjustment are the same. Once active intervention by the central bank in the foreign exchange market is no longer needed, or when the exchange rate is stable without intervention, private net foreign demand for assets are equal to net export levels. The current account and financial markets are intimately linked. Changes in either have repercussions in the other.

Reduction in the level of domestic investment in Japan leads to slower Japanese real growth. It also leads to greater Japanese net foreign investment and higher net exports. As such, it can be seen as a major contributor to Japan's increased foreign direct investment, Japan's role as the major creditor nation, and Japan's large trade surpluses.

REDUCTION OF PROTECTIONISM IN JAPAN

Even if Japan abolished all protectionist barriers facing Japanese imports, the long-term effects would not result in a significantly reduced Japanese trade surplus. The best estimates of the increased imports by Japan if all trade barriers were removed and nothing else changed are between $5 and $8 billion (Bergsten and Cline, 1985, p. 114). The liberalization would, however, set into motion a whole series of adjustments which, at constant savings, investment, taxing, and government spending levels, would lead to a relatively small change in the overall trade balance.

If Japan increased imports by $10 billion, the short-term effect would be to lower the amount of Japanese output through the multiplier effect. The reduction in Japanese net exports would also tend to weaken demand for the yen. The lower aggregate demand would perhaps lead to lower Japanese prices. With a weakened yen and lower prices, Japanese goods would be more competitive in the global market.

The amount of Japanese exports would increase. This would occur as output in the previously protected sector declined. Resources that were previously used to produce rice and other protected commodities would now be used to produce other goods. Some of the other goods produced would be export goods. If the amount of net demand for foreign assets stayed constant, then the extra export earnings by the United States, Canada, Australia, Brazil, and others would be available for purchase of additional Japanese goods. Also, the extra net exports to Japan by these countries would tend to increase their aggregate expenditures. The value of the foreign currencies would be likely to rise. These tendencies would be likely to raise the relative prices of foreign goods. This would tend to make goods produced in the United States and other countries exporting to Japan less competitive. Thus, these countries' imports would tend to increase. Their exports of goods other than the liberalized items would be likely to fall. Likewise, Japanese imports of goods other than the liberalized goods would probably fall.

The overall change in Japan's net trade position is likely to be fairly small due to liberalization. The principal long-term effects would be to increase the welfare of Japanese consumers. Global producers of restricted products, primarily food and agriculture, would benefit. Japanese agricultural owners and workers would suffer negative consequences. Both the positive and negative consequences would be greater in Japan than in the rest of the world. This is because Japan's relative prices now are further than relative prices in the world market from what relative prices would be with complete liberalization. Liberalization should be carried out, but it is not a solution to the trade balance problem. It would primarily benefit Japanese consumers.

SHIFT IN JAPANESE PORTFOLIO HOLDINGS

Changes in Japanese financial regulations in the 1970s and 1980s permitted greater international capital inflows and outflows. As a consequence, capital flows in both directions increased, especially in the 1980s.

The increases were lopsided, however, in the direction of greater capital outflow. While there are conflicting arguments, one reason for this might be because of a pent-up demand for foreign assets on the part of Japanese life insurance companies and other large institutional investors (Lincoln, 1988, pp. 247–49).

A sudden shift in Japanese portfolio preferences could have major consequences for Japan and for other countries. If there were a shift of preferences (or a change in regulations) of the Japanese in favor of additional holdings of foreign assets, it would affect Japanese and foreign asset returns and valuation exchange rates, Japanese and foreign investments, Japanese and foreign income levels, and trade flows. A reversal of such preferences would cause changes in the opposite direction.

If Japanese institutions wanted to quickly increase foreign assets in their portfolios, they would need to sell Japanese securities and buy foreign securities. Since the United States is the major recipient of Japanese investment, the remaining discussion will be in terms of the United States and Japan. The actual changes that took place in Japanese institutional portfolio adjustments were more gradual, and took the form of increasing the proportion of investment in foreign assets. The intent here is to show the changes from the base case, without the change in preference, even though Japanese institutions actually continued to add domestic assets to their portfolios.

The immediate effect of the portfolio change would be to raise asset prices in the United States and to lower asset prices in Japan. Since asset prices are simply the risk-adjusted present value of future coupons, dividends, or earnings, this is equivalent to saying the rate of discount would be lower in the United States and higher in Japan, at least with the initial simplifying assumption of no change in dividends or earnings because of the shift.

Let us follow the transactions involved in a little greater detail, and look for connections to other markets. Suppose a Japanese life insurance company sells 239 million yen worth of Japanese government bonds. They convert the proceeds of the sale to dollars at 239 yen per dollar (the rate in 1985), for one million U.S. dollars. They use that million dollars to buy a million dollars worth of U.S. Treasury bonds. As time passes, the interest on the U.S. bonds will be paid out to the Japanese life insurance company in dollars, and probably converted into yen for payouts to policy holders.

The purchase of U.S. Treasury bonds would constitute an increase in demand for these bonds, and would tend to drive up their price. The sale of Japanese Treasury bonds would constitute a net decrease in demand for these bonds, and would tend to drive down their price. The same number of bonds would still exist in both countries and they would still be owned by someone. Of course, a million dollars is such a small amount in these markets that this hypothetical transaction would not affect much. However, if many Japanese institutions were making these changes, cumulatively their transactions would have great impact. Also, a single institution could well deal in the hundreds of millions of dollars, which could have an impact individually. The foreign exchange transactions directly involved would tend to cause the spot price of the U.S. dollar to rise and the forward price of the dollar to fall.

The need to convert yen to U.S. dollars to buy the U.S. Treasury bonds would be an increase in demand for dollars on the spot exchange market. The spot exchange market is the market for foreign currency for immediate transactions (within 3 days). This increase in demand would tend to increase the price of dollars in the spot foreign exchange market. The probability of more dollars being converted to yen in the future as interest payments are made would tend to lower the expected price of dollars in the future. Everything else the same, this should lower the price of the dollar in the forward exchange market. The forward exchange market is the market for foreign currency transactions at some future stipulated date. The contract is entered into now for the future transaction.

Large international banks monitor the relationship among interest rates and spot and forward exchange rates virtually all the time. They are prepared to undertake certain arbitrage activities whenever the opportunity for profits without increased risk occurs. This activity is called covered interest arbitrage. Covered interest arbitrage ensures that, within a narrow band, if regulations do not prevent it, there will be an equality between the ratio of one plus the Japanese interest rate and one plus the U.S. interest rate, and the ratio of the forward exchange rate (yen per dollar) and the spot exchange rate. The forward rate and the interest rate are stipulated for the same time period. When this equality holds, covered interest parity is said to hold.

Covered interest arbitragers would act to restore covered interest parity if a portfolio shift caused a disturbance in the relationship. Examining the ratio of interest rates, we note that Japanese rates would rise and U.S. rates would fall because of the portfolio adjustment. Thus, the ratio of Japanese to U.S. rates would rise due to the portfolio adjustment. Examining the ratio of the forward exchange rate to the spot exchange rate, we note that the forward rate would tend to fall and the spot rate would tend to rise. The ratio of the forward rate to the spot rate would thus tend to fall due to the portfolio adjustment.

With the interest rate ratio rising and the forward to spot ratio falling, covered interest arbitragers would shift their holdings from U.S. Treasury bills to Japanese Treasury bills, while buying yen in the spot market and selling yen on the forward market. These activities would tend to raise U.S. Treasury bill rates and lower Japanese Treasury bill rates. The transactions would also tend to raise the forward rate for the dollar and lower the spot rate for the dollar. Since covered interest arbitragers act in the market where coverage of the exchange risk can be obtained, they would affect short-term rates more directly. The result would be a lessening of the normal premium that is obtained on long-term bond holdings in the United States, and an increase in the premium in the Japanese market. Also, covered interest arbitragers would actually undertake forward contracts to sell yen at various maturity dates in the near future. The tendency noted earlier for higher expectations of yen purchases in order to return bond interest to Japan may not lead to actual forward contracts. If there were not sufficiently strong speculative demand, the value of the forward yen would be likely to decline, that is, the forward yen to dollar exchange rate would rise. The net outcome for any given interest or exchange rate is unknown. Part of the result would depend on policy responses. In a fixed exchange rate regime, all the changes would be in interest rates and relative money supplies.

There are two main avenues whereby the change in portfolio preference would result in changes in trade flows between Japan and the United States. The first is the increased consumption that would occur because of the higher perceived wealth in the United States. The second is from the stimulus to investment that would come from lower real interest rates in the United States.

The increased perceived wealth in the United States would come from two sources. First is the higher price of U.S. assets in dollar terms as Japanese life insurance companies bought U.S. assets. Second, as the spot exchange rate rose, it would cost more yen to buy a dollar's worth of assets. Consequently, a given investor in the United States evaluating her wealth in terms of how many of the world's goods she could buy would conclude that she was richer than before the portfolio adjustment. This higher perceived wealth would likely lead to higher spending on consumption. Since some consumption spending falls on foreign goods and services, the U.S. trade balance would deteriorate.

The lower U.S. real interest rates due to the portfolio change in Japan would tend to stimulate investment. If the United States had unemployed resources, as it did in 1985, then the resulting increase in aggregate expenditure would increase real income, pursuant to the Keynesian multiplier effect. Increased expenditure would also tend to increase upward pressure on prices, thus increasing inflationary pressure. Increased income means increased consumption, some of which would be consumption of foreign goods and services. Some of the investment spending would also be on foreign equipment. Price increases of U.S. goods and the higher value of the dollar would both make U.S. goods and services less competitive in the global market. After a delay, this would cause the U.S. trade balance to deteriorate.

MACROECONOMIC INFLUENCES OF JAPAN

Three changes that have occurred in Japan's economy that have had effects on the rest of the world have been explored in this chapter. Each change has implications beyond its immediate effects. The linkages traced here have been rather complicated. The full effects in the real world are even more complex. Matters are further complicated by the overlapping of different changes in underlying conditions and policies in Japan and in the rest of the world. Nevertheless, some insights can be gained by examining macroeconomic effects.

The slowdown in the growth of the Japanese economy has been a major factor contributing to Japan's trade surpluses in the 1980s. The liberalization of Japan's financial markets and consequent foreign investment by Japanese insurance companies and other Japanese financial institutions have also contributed to Japan's trade surplus. Real rates of return in Japan on financial investment have been lower than in most developed economies in the last two decades, but they would probably have been lower still if Japanese financial capital had been restricted to the domestic economy. Likewise, the real rate of return on U.S. financial capital, while very high in the 1980s, would have been higher if not for Japanese financial investment.

U.S. borrowing and Japanese lending are the primary reasons for the massive U.S. trade deficits and Japanese trade surpluses. The changes have been primarily the result of Reagan policies in the United States, which we will explore in chapter 7, and the availability of Japanese funds as a result of Japan's slower growth and liberalization. Japanese trade barriers have played no substantive role in causing the present trade imbalances. Virtually all Japanese trade barriers were existing long before the large Japanese surpluses began. Further, liberalization of these barriers, while desirable, would by themselves have little effect on Japanese trade balances.

Japan has had an increasingly important impact on the rest of the global economy. In 1955, Japanese gross domestic product (GDP) was 3 percent of the GDP of all of the market economies. By 1985, Japan's GDP was 12 percent of the total. This means a change in Japan's rate of growth or trade has four times the relative impact of thirty years ago. Changes are even greater in the relative importance of Japan when measured by relative financial markets. At the end of 1987, Japan's market valuation of stocks was 42 percent of the world market, compared with 31 percent for the United States (Honeygold, 1989, p. 55). Such relative valuations change with fluctuations in exchange rates and market gains and losses. Nevertheless, it is undeniable that Japan has become an ever more important global power. Japanese leaders should consider the impact on the rest of the global economy when selecting appropriate policy measures.

7 MACROECONOMIC EFFECTS OF THE GLOBAL ECONOMY ON JAPAN

There have been a number of economic events in the post–World War II period originating outside of Japan that have had major effects on Japan's economy. The Korean and Vietnam wars both had repercussions on Japan as a supply center and staging area. The collapse of the Bretton-Woods fixed exchange rate system has affected all countries in the global economy, including Japan. The oil crises in 1973–74 and 1979–80 dramatically changed Japan's terms of trade and disrupted the Japanese economy. The Reagan deficits in the United States and debt crises in Latin America and Eastern Europe have shifted conditions facing Japanese financial markets and caused changes in trade patterns. The opening of China to freer commerce and moves by the Soviet Union in that direction have important implications for the Japanese economy. The organization of the European Economic Community (EEC) has had an impact on Japan also, even though its primary focus has been on the countries in the EEC.

This chapter explores two of these events in some depth, so that the mechanisms connecting changes in one area to other economic areas can be better understood. This is especially important in understanding policy choices. The first event to be explored is the effect of the sudden rise in oil prices. The second will be the Reagan deficits in the United States. There are times when policymakers blame other parties, especially other countries, for the ultimate effects of their own decisions. I believe this has happened in the case of the Reagan deficits.

THE EFFECTS OF A MAJOR RISE IN OIL PRICES ON JAPAN

Petroleum and petroleum products are a major portion of Japan's imports. In 1987, as we saw in table 3.3, 15 percent of Japan's imports were crude petroleum and another 5 percent were petroleum products. These percentages were in value terms, and thus reflected the relatively low level of oil prices in 1987. In 1975, 36 percent of the value of Japanese imports were imports of petroleum and petroleum products. Another 9 percent were imports of other fuels whose prices are tied to oil prices through substitution effects. Consequently, a change in the price of oil represents a change in the terms of trade of Japan.

A rise in the price of oil constitutes a deterioration of Japan's terms of trade. The effects of this worsening of Japan's terms of trade can be broken down into the long-run effects on the assumption of a permanent change and the short-run effects of dislocation and adjustment that are likely to occur. The long-run effects on Japan include a reduction in welfare and an increase in the quantity of exports. The short-run transitional effects are higher inflation, a reduced trade surplus, and a possible recession.

The Long-Run General Equilibrium Effects of an Oil Price Rise

An increase in Japan's import price of oil brought about by changes outside Japan definitely reduces welfare in Japan. It is possible for Japan to be better off even with higher import prices if prices change because of a higher rate of growth in Japan or some other cause originating in Japan. When the change is in the rest of the world, though, there are no offsetting benefits for Japan. Thus, Japan is definitely worse off.

In the jargon of international trade theory, Japan's offer curve is unchanged and the offer curve of the oil-exporting countries has moved nearer the origin. Japan's trade position is nearer the origin along its offer curve and Japan is definitely worse off. One can think of it as being forced to be closer to the position of no international trade. Japan thus loses some of the benefits of trade that it had enjoyed.

In terms of consumption, the effect is the same as if money income were held constant and the price of a major consumption item were increased. Regardless of how the consumers adjusted their spending patterns, they could not achieve the same level of well-being that they enjoyed prior to the price change. The effects on Japan are more complicated than the case of the consumer, because of adjustments to production and trading patterns. Nevertheless, the end result on welfare is the same. The Japanese are made worse off by the change.

The basic long-run adjustment to an increase in the price of oil runs somewhat as follows. Consumers of oil substitute away from the more expensive product and buy more of other goods that are now less expensive. Falling real income reduces consumption of all goods. Production shifts to produce more energy and use less of it. Japanese imports of oil fall, but probably not very much. The quantity of Japanese exports will probably increase.

At a given real income, nonenergy goods will be in greater demand because of the substitution away from higher priced energy goods. Especially affected by this substitution will be other fuels like coal and natural gas, which will also rise in price because of this higher demand. Oil price rises thus tend to cause an increase in all energy prices.

Real income does not, however, stay constant. As oil prices rise, Japanese real income falls. As Japanese real income falls, Japanese consumers buy fewer goods of all types. A priori, we do not know whether the substitution effect or income effect will dominate in Japan. Theoretically, it is possible for Japanese nonenergy consumption to either increase or decrease because of a rise in oil prices. Energy demand tends to have a low elasticity of demand, which would result in less consumption of nonenergy items.

There will be a shift in the goods produced in Japan and in the way in which goods are produced. The increased price of energy relative to other goods produced in the Japanese economy will lead producers to increase the amount of energy produced. Unfortunately for Japan, it has virtually no oil resources. Its coal output will probably increase, but will continue to be a small percentage of total consumption. There will probably be a significant rise in nuclear power generation in Japan, as long as the oil price rise is considered to be permanent. Present nuclear generation is about 9 percent of Japan's total energy use (Chandler and Brauchli, 1990). Since there will not likely be much shift of resources into producing more energy in Japan due to the limited opportunities, there will not be much reduction in production of other goods because of such dislocations.

Major changes in the mix of goods produced in Japan will come about because of the higher cost of oil as an input in the production process and because the new pattern of demand might be different from the old pattern. Goods that have a high energy content, such as chemicals and fertilizers, will rise in price relative to many other goods if oil prices rise. Consequently, the quantity of such goods demanded will be lower. Relatively more of the goods with low energy content will be demanded and produced in Japan, and in other countries as well. Also, reduced demand occurs for goods that use a lot of energy in their operation, such as cars.

Those countries with net exports of oil will have increases in their real incomes, and thus will increase their imports of all kinds of goods. Other countries that are net importers of oil, like Japan, will reduce their nonenergy imports due to lower real income. It is unlikely that the substitution effect is strong enough to outweigh this effect of lower real income. The United Kingdom, Norway, and the Soviet Union are exceptions, but most of the oil-exporting countries do not have a large industrial base. They will primarily be importing final consumption goods, rather than the machine tools and intermediate goods that are imported by the United States and the European Community. The shift in demand will cause Japan and other industrial countries to produce more of the goods demanded by the oil-exporting countries and less of those goods demanded by the oil-importing countries.

The production processes used in Japan and elsewhere will change to economize on the now more expensive oil and other energy. There will be an immediate shift to use less energy-intensive techniques that are already known, if they result in cheaper output at the higher price of energy. Other changes may not occur until existing machinery is replaced. Such replacement will tend to be accelerated by a major change in any input price, including energy.

Research and development in Japan and globally will focus on ways to economize on oil and other energy when oil prices rise. It was largely through such economizing that the real price of oil was forced back down after the 1979–80 price rises. Use of energy out of each extra dollar of U.S. real gross national product (GNP) declined by 28 percent from 1972 to 1989 (Energy Information Administration, 1990). Japan's savings on energy use have been even greater (Chandler and Brauchli, 1990). This has tended to reverse earlier price rises. Of course, once the improved energy technology is developed, firms do not discard it when oil prices fall back.

Japanese imports of oil at a given GNP will fall as a consequence of the changes that have been discussed. The direct substitution away from using oil because of its price rise reduces consumption of oil. Using fewer goods that use oil in the production process or in their operation will also reduce consumption of oil. The improvement in production processes to economize on oil will reduce total demand for oil. Oil imports, however, are not likely to fall by much. Substitution possibilities for oil are fairly limited. The elasticity of long-run demand (ten year adjustment) for oil appears to be about –.404 (Baldwin and Prosser, 1988). This means that for a 10 percent increase in the relative price of oil, use of oil will fall by 4.04 percent over a ten year period. The short-run response will be even less. Since oil imports will not fall by as high a percentage as prices rise, more goods will have to be exported from Japan to pay for its oil imports.

Of course, most oil-importing countries will be going through many of these same adjustments at pretty much the same time. The adjustments will affect those variables that we assume will be constant or irrelevant in a long-run equilibrium. There will be pressures on employment, investment, government budgets, trade balances, interest rates, price levels, asset values, and exchange rates.

The Short-Run Macroeconomic Effects of an Oil Price Rise

A sharp rise in oil prices would have major impacts on the macroeconomy of Japan. Such a price rise would tend to lower Japan's trade surplus. Japan would probably experience higher inflation. The yen would probably weaken with a rise in oil prices. Japan could experience a contraction, either a growth recession or an absolute recession. Japanese asset values would probably decline. There would probably be fluctuations in interest rates, both nominal and real. The Japanese government deficit would probably worsen because of an oil price rise.

The most direct and obvious effect of higher oil prices on Japan would be a worsening of its trade balance. "Worsening" is used here in its traditional meaning, indicating a lower trade surplus or greater trade deficit. Actually, in the case of Japan in 1990, decreasing Japan's trade surplus is an announced policy of the Japanese government. Of course, the Japanese would like to lower the trade surplus as the result of increased consumption of goods and services. In that way they would be achieving a higher standard of living. Increasing the price paid for oil imports would reduce Japan's trade surplus without any concomitant increase in Japan's welfare.

It is not clear what the follow-up response to the higher oil price would be on the trade balance. The higher price raises consumption costs to the Japanese. If they seek to maintain the same percentage savings rate as previously, they will have to cut their consumption of other goods. If the level of investment stays constant, the Japanese trade balance might return approximately to its original position. Nonetheless, given Japan's current policy of reducing its trade surplus, a rise in oil prices might assist in accomplishing this goal.

The direct effect of an oil price increase is to increase the price level. The only way the price level can stay constant is if nonenergy prices fall to offset the rise in energy prices. Given that prices of many goods are sticky, prices of other goods are not likely to fall enough, and inflation will probably be worse because of oil price hikes. Sticky prices occur largely when firms adjust output rather than prices when there is a decrease in demand. In the oil shock of 1973–74, Japan adopted a policy response of rapid money growth, which resulted in a high level of inflation. In 1979–80, Japanese policymakers adopted a slower money growth stance without nearly as much inflation. They evidently concluded that a high rate of inflation did not assist the adjustment process very much (Suzuki, 1986, pp. 132–34).

Most oil exports are denominated in U.S. dollars. As a result, an increase in oil prices raises the amount of international trade that is invoiced in dollars. This raises the demand for U.S. dollars, and will (everything else the same) raise the value of the dollar relative to other currencies, including the yen. The weakening yen is another way for Japan to reach a higher level of exports to pay for its oil if it continues at its present level of trade surplus. If Japanese inflation rises more than the dollar, that too could cause a weakening of the yen. The major international currencies (dollar, yen, and deutsche mark) are from countries that are net oil importers. Of the major currencies, only the pound sterling is a currency of an oil exporter. Consequently, it is hard to predict how the attempt to increase exports to pay for oil imports will affect the relative strength of the different currencies. It is only the dollar's connection to invoicing of oil trade that contributes to its strength. Britain's pound should also strengthen as its greater oil revenue in dollars is converted into pounds. The final outcome of currency realignments will depend on the various policies adopted by the countries involved.

A rise in oil prices might cause an economic contraction in Japan, due to the wealth effect and the difficulty in quickly expanding exports. Since Japanese real income falls when oil prices rise, in the present period and for as long as oil prices stay higher, the Japanese would correctly see this as a loss of real wealth. That is, the present value of their future real income stream will be lower than before if the oil price rise is unexpected.

Japanese citizens will respond to lower wealth and real income with reduced consumption and increased saving at a given level of income. Unfortunately, when everyone tries to save more at the same time, the result can be a fall in income as firms are unable to sell all of the output they are producing. In macroeconomic textbooks this is sometimes referred to as the "paradox of thrift" (Lipsey and Steiner, 1981, pp. 526–27). As noted earlier, one of the alternatives to reducing output is to increase export sales. However, the increased desire to save because of lower wealth and expected real income would also occur in all the countries that are net importers of oil. It will be hard for any country, including Japan, to increase exports to oil importers.

The oil-exporting countries may not quickly expand their imports. The extra oil revenue generated by the higher prices may be saved in large part. Even when these revenues are used to repay accumulated debts, they do not have the needed effect of maintaining global demand for the level of global output. If Japan's domestic demand falls and demand for Japan's exports falls also, or just does not rise as much as domestic demand falls, then Japan could enter a recessionary spiral.

Asset values in Japan will probably decline when oil prices rise. Asset values are the risk-adjusted present value of claims on future payments or earnings. There are a number of ways they are affected by oil price increases.

Expected earnings will decline because Japanese firms will have been trying to maximize profits before the price rise with combinations of capital, labor, and energy that were most efficient at the old prices. Changing these production processes is time consuming and costly. In the meantime, Japanese firms will be producing at less than maximum efficiency. Of course, firms in other countries will be going through the same process. Nevertheless, the earnings of the firms will be adversely affected during this transition period.

Japanese interest rates will fluctuate a lot because of an oil price rise. The actual level will depend in large part on the Bank of Japan, but a number of forces will be operating. Real short-run interest rates will likely fall because of the increased desire of residents to save. Also, firms will probably pause in their investment spending until they evaluate the changes that are required due to the new higher level of oil prices. Unlike the United States and other countries with significant oil resources, Japan will not have major investments in domestic energy exploration to partially offset this slump in short-term investment. Further out in time, the short-term real interest rate should approach its initial position, if Japan is in equilibrium at the time oil prices rise.

Long-run real interest rates are likely to rise due to the oil price shock. This is largely because of the increased inflationary pressure mentioned before. Higher inflationary expectations with a high degree of uncertainty attached are likely to require a higher premium for holding long-term assets even beyond the increased expectation of inflation. This is especially true if higher real short-term rates are expected in the future.

The uncertainty about earnings is also likely to require a higher equity premium than before. Long-term investors in stocks are likely to require a higher expected real return on stock holdings compared to expected real returns on long-term bonds.

The Japanese government deficit will probably worsen with an increase in the price of oil. If a contraction in the economy occurs, the government will probably stimulate the economy with an increase in government spending or a decrease in taxes. Also, because the government is a net debtor, any increase in interest rates will increase the nominal deficit.

Most of the impact felt by Japan from a higher price of oil will also fall on any other oil-importing country. The United States is better off than Japan in adjusting to oil price changes, since the United States has large oil, gas, and coal supplies. Many European countries are totally dependent on oil imports, like Japan. It is, in fact, this similarity of adjustment problems that makes a sharp oil price increase so dangerous to macroeconomic stability. One obvious solution for most countries in the face of domestic weakness is to export more. However, every nation cannot increase net exports at the same time.

THE EFFECTS OF U.S. DEFICITS ON JAPAN

The Reagan deficits in the 1980s were caused by tax cuts and defense increases. These deficits lowered the U.S. net national savings and stimulated consumer spending. Foreign financial flows into the United States were encouraged by the increase in the U.S. real interest rates. These financial flows tended to raise the value of the dollar and (with a lag) reduced the growth in U.S. exports and increased the growth in U.S. imports. U.S. manufacturers lost market share at home and abroad. It was a combination of U.S. fiscal and monetary policy that brought about unprecedented foreign trade deficits that have yet to be reversed.

Japan has been a major exporter to and importer from the United States throughout this period. As U.S. exports fell generally, they also fell to Japan. U.S. imports from Japan increased sharply, and Japan has been a major provider of international financial resources. As mentioned in chapter 6, Japan's rate of domestic investment was falling during the early 1980s. The result was an increase in Japan's global trade surplus and a dramatic rise in Japan's bilateral surplus with the United States.

The Long-Run General Equilibrium Effects of the Reagan Deficits

The long-run effects of the Reagan deficits result from the redistribution of government spending and tax liabilities. The wisdom or foolishness of Reagan's defense buildup is largely a function of whether one accepts the idea that the Soviet Union's moves toward arms control were largely or slightly influenced by the U.S. arms buildup. If largely influenced, then the buildup is likely to pay off handsomely, even in an economic sense, if the Cold War is indeed over. From the analytical view of the deficits, though, it is the size of total government consumption spending, not its composition, that is important.

The essential nature of the Reagan deficits was a tax cut that persisted throughout the business cycle. The economy, even at full employment, would generate a government deficit. Since government spending, albeit on different priorities, continued apace, tax receipts were inadequate to pay for expenditures. The government borrowed the difference. Most of the borrowing was from U.S. residents, but an unprecedented amount came from and continues to come from foreigners.

The burden of government borrowing is sometimes said to be a burden on future generations. This holds true when the borrowing is from foreigners, in the sense that future U.S. residents will have to curtail consumption to repay the borrowed funds. The foreign borrowing permits total national expenditures to exceed output. The difference is the current account deficit. Unless our economy continuously expands at a faster pace than foreign economies, at some point the debt must be repaid. We must then ship more to foreigners than they ship to us. That is the burden on future generations of Americans. They must reduce consumption below what it would otherwise be to transfer resources back to our lenders.

The internal effect of government borrowing is different in its distributional effects. For a given level of output, an increase in government spending on goods and services must necessarily reduce spending on other goods and services. If the trade balance stays constant, then the only areas for reduction are consumption expenditures and investment expenditures. The real present burden of government spending is this foregone consumption and investment. The distribution of this burden is generally quite different when government spending is financed by taxes or borrowings. The overall level of the burden that is borne by the present generation is basically the same regardless of which way the spending is financed. One of the economic functions of policymakers is to ensure that government spending provides sufficient public welfare to justify the burden of foregone consumption and investment.

The differences in the distributional effects of taxing versus borrowing are important. Borrowing is likely to lower investment spending relative to consumption. Borrowing also tends to benefit those citizens who have money to lend and harm those who are net borrowers in the society. These effects are due to the general result that when the government borrows instead of taxing, for a given level of spending, the level of the real interest rate is higher. Higher real interest rates tend to reduce investment in plant and equipment and to give a higher income to those who are net lenders.

In many instances, those who pay lower income taxes because of the Reagan tax cuts also lend the government money. They may buy government bonds and bills directly, or through mutual funds or other financial institutions. An economic proposition called "Ricardian equivalence" maintains that rational taxpayers recognize that government borrowing incurs future liabilities and treat it as a deferred tax. In the aggregate, for all taxpayers, the obligation of the government's borrowing exists. The government will either have to repay the loan at some point in time or continue paying interest on the loan indefinitely. However, the individual's tax burden in the future is not known.

The well-to-do in the American economy who had their marginal tax rates on property income cut from 70 percent to 28 percent during the Reagan years are likely to believe that, when taxes are increased to repay or service the debt incurred, their rates will not return to the original level. Others in the American economy who are not so fortunate may feel relieved at a small decline in their tax rate. They fail to realize that the loan they get on their car might cost them an extra $200 per year or their home loan an extra $2,000 per year because of government tax cuts. Even worse, because of the tax cuts, they may not be able to afford the house or the car. Financing costs are the most important component of housing, and are very important in automobile purchases as well. Many voters fail to realize the connection, and do not blame the Reagan borrowing for reducing their consumption and investment just as surely as taxes would have. When the general equilibrium effects are tallied up, it is very likely that the overall consumption levels of taxpayers who were major net borrowers were lower in the 1980s because of the Reagan deficits. In the future, when taxes are increased to reduce the deficit or service the accumulated debt, they are likely to have their consumption further reduced. Taxpayers who are large net lenders in the United States have benefitted from higher interest rates during the deficit years. It is likely that when taxes are increased they will still have benefitted overall from the Reagan tax cuts and deficits. This is especially true if they were in the upper income groups that had the largest cuts in taxes.

The Short-Run Macroeconomic Effects of the Reagan Deficits

The 1981 Reagan income tax cuts were stimulative in nature and as such helped the United States recover from the 1981–82 recession. The continuation of large deficit spending with a tight money policy and flexible exchange rate led to large deficits in the balance of trade. These trade deficits tended to restrict wage gains and reductions in unemployment. This caused a very uneven sharing of the burden of adjustment. There were also painful adjustments required that necessarily had to be undone. This was wasteful and caused unnecessary suffering. The Japanese have been blamed for the resulting trade imbalances that were largely brought about by U.S. government policy.

When an economy is not fully utilizing its productive resources, a tax cut can lead to increases in output. This is especially true when the tax cut, like that in 1981 in the United States, accelerates tax depreciation of equipment and real estate. The faster depreciation permits postponement of taxation, and thereby makes investment in such assets more appealing. Having more after-tax income available leads to more saving and more consumption. The increase in consumption leads to higher aggregate demand. Firms hire more workers as they can sell more of their output. The new hires and the greater confidence of existing workers lead to more consumption spending. The end result is a higher level of output in the economy. Looked at over time, economic growth is faster than it would have been.

As an economy nears full employment, increases in aggregate spending lead to increases in prices rather than increases in output. In a more elaborate analysis, everything can be recast in terms of changes that occur faster than expected. Unexpected changes in fiscal and monetary policy would tend to have the impacts described here as simple changes. When an economy is at or near full employment, physical output can only grow over time as the labor supply, capital, and technology increase. It is usually at this phase of the business cycle that labor makes its greatest relative gains. Frequently, profits are squeezed. Capital spending plans are cut, and a recession begins. Often, it is the interest-sensitive sector of the economy, housing and automobiles, that leads the nation into recession as the central bank increases interest rates to cool the economy's growth.

The Reagan deficit period was affected by tight U.S. monetary policy and flexible exchange rates. The Federal Reserve (Fed) was trying, from 1979 on, to sharply lower the rate of inflation and the expectation of inflation. To do this, the Fed announced the policy goal of money supply growth, and its intention to let interest rates rise if necessary. It was this policy, together with entrenched inflationary expectations and the 1979–80 oil price hikes, that led to the 1981–82 recession in the United States. This recession was the worst in the United States since the Great Depression in the 1930s.

As the Reagan tax cuts and defense buildup kicked in, the U.S. economy grew from its low point in 1982. As the economy grew, U.S. imports grew more quickly than exports. The trade deficits had to be financed by foreign borrowings. At a fixed exchange rate, the growth in the United States due to the large fiscal stimulus would have led fairly quickly to full employment and inflationary pressures. There would have been a rise in real interest rates in order to attract foreign capital. At some fairly early point, the fiscal stimulus would have needed to be reduced.

The actual developments in the United States were more complex and were evidently misunderstood at the highest levels of the Reagan administration. The dollar generally appreciated over the 1981–85 period. By 1985, the U.S. dollar was 5 percent stronger against the yen, 62 percent stronger against the deutsche mark, and 17 percent stronger against the Canadian dollar. This dollar strength was in spite of the increasing U.S. trade deficits, which had risen from .5 percent of GNP in 1980 to 3 percent of GNP by 1985.

Normally, a trade deficit could be expected to weaken a currency, which should eventually lead to greater competitiveness of the country's goods and services in global markets. The continued tightness of the Fed kept U.S. interest rates high, and the momentum of dollar appreciation continued to cause the dollar to strengthen further. Under Donald Regan at the U.S. Treasury, the Reagan administration refused to intervene to stop the rising dollar and refused to take policy action to reverse its course. Reagan and Regan even took pride in how strong the dollar was.

The problem was that U.S. manufacturers were becoming very uncompetitive globally because of the overvalued dollar (McKinnon, 1987, p. 368). U.S. exports as a percentage of GNP fell from 10.2 percent in 1980 to 7.1 percent in 1985. Imports also fell as a percentage of GNP from 10.7 percent to 10.1 percent, which is a much more modest decline. Imports rose from the 9.5 percent of GNP level in 1982. Exports were 8.7 percent of GNP in 1982, and continued to fall as a percentage. As is well known, the Reagan trade deficits transformed the United States from the world's largest creditor nation to the world's largest debtor nation.

The United States cannot run a trade deficit without other countries running a trade surplus. The principal trade surplus countries are those that have relatively high savings rates like Japan and Germany. Nevertheless, it seems clear that the major changes have occurred in the United States. It is up to the United States to reverse the decline in the national savings rate due to the government deficits. Net savings in the United States in 1980–87 fell to 3.7 percent of GNP, from 7.7 percent of GNP in 1974–79. Net savings were thus only 39 percent of what they were in the earlier period. Japan's net savings also fell during the 1980–87 period, but only to 17.6 percent, from 20.2 percent in 1974–79. Germany's rate fell from 11.5 percent in 1974–79 to 9.5 percent in 1980–87. The changes in Japan and Germany did not cause the U.S. deficits, they merely responded to them. To blame Japan for U.S. trade deficits is a lot like blaming your banker because you are in debt.

SUMMARY

Japan is subject to shocks to its economic system that originate in other countries or regions. The oil price shocks of 1973–74 and 1979–80 are examples of such shocks. The Reagan deficits are another disturbance with effects on Japan.

Rising oil prices tend to lower Japan's real income. Japan's production shifts toward producing more goods demanded by oil-exporting countries instead of importing countries when oil prices rise. The adjustment of an individual country like Japan is complicated by the simultaneous changes going on in other importing countries.

Oil price increases tend to reduce Japanese asset prices. Inflationary pressure in Japan increases. Japan's trade surplus is reduced directly by oil price rises. Japan could enter a recessionary period as higher interest rates, uncertainty, and lower trade balances put downward pressure on the economy. Japan's policy response in 1979–80 to the oil shock successfully avoided inflationary consequences.

Increases in U.S. deficits during the Reagan years substantially lowered the U.S. national savings rate. As a consequence, the United States ran large and persistent trade deficits. Tight monetary policy in the United States strengthened the dollar and continued to attract capital flows from around the world, in spite of these large deficits. The United States has been transformed from the world's largest creditor nation to its largest debtor nation. It still has not extricated itself from this dilemma.

Japan has been a major source of financial flows to the United States. It has run persistent trade surpluses during the 1980s. Japan has been the banker to the United States. The United States needs to stop borrowing abroad if it wants to return to balance of payments equilibrium.

8 JAPANESE INVESTMENT ABROAD

Economists usually use the term *investment* to mean plant and equipment used in the production process. Common usage of the term refers to purchase of existing financial assets ranging from bank accounts to stocks, bonds, and futures contracts. The physical investment referred to by economists underlies the financial investments commonly referred to. International capital flows are most directly related to the common definition of investment. When foreigners buy more of domestic financial assets than they sell, there is an inflow of foreign capital. This can take place regardless of what is happening to economic investment in the domestic economy for a given period of time. This chapter is devoted to exploring how Japanese investment in foreign economies has developed over the postwar period, and what the near future might bring.

The general motivations for financial investments at home and abroad are developed in this chapter. The relationships that should prevail in an efficient international capital market are reviewed, including arbitrage and allocational efficiency. Japan's total foreign investment and its components in recent years are presented and discussed. Japanese foreign direct investment by country is presented for the postwar period, and determinants of regional shares are discussed. Japanese foreign direct investment by industry for the postwar period is also presented and discussed.

GLOBAL INVESTING

The basic act of making a financial investment is an attempt to make an intertemporal economic exchange. An individual buys a financial instrument today with the expectation of receiving certain benefits at some point in the future. The money exchanged at the present time represents generalized purchasing power that could have been used for current consumption. It is the forgoing of current consumption that frees up the real economic resources that can then be used for investment in new production capabilities.

The individual or institution selling the financial instrument may be planning to use the money received to undertake the construction of plant or equipment and thereby increase productive capacity. Alternatively, the seller might use the money to increase current consumption. When an owner of an existing financial asset, like a bond, sells the asset, the seller may increase consumption or reinvest the proceeds into a different type of asset. Most financial asset sales and purchases net out. It is the changes in asset levels that have a large economic impact. Nevertheless, the existence of an active and organized market that permits low-cost trades of existing assets contributes to the flow of current resources into real investment in productive capacity.

The return on ownership interests in productive capacity and the preferences of economic agents for consumption today versus likely consumption in the future largely determine the prices at which financial assets trade. If the likely return on ownership interests falls, then prices of those ownership interests will fall, all else the same. If economic agents increase their desire for future consumption relative to today's consumption, they will be willing to pay more for financial assets, and prices of such assets will rise.

The future payoff of financial assets is uncertain. This uncertainty causes many complications in the pricing and exchange of financial assets. Some major uncertainties include:

1. The buyer of the asset not knowing if he will be alive to enjoy the expected consumption;
2. The possible default of the seller of the asset;
3. The possible change in the nominal value of the asset during the holding period; and
4. The possible change in what the proceeds from the asset will buy at the end of the holding period.

Generally speaking, the lower the uncertainties involved in owning a financial asset, the closer will be its price now and its expected price at the end of the holding period. Another way of putting this is that the lower the risk, the lower the expected return will have to be to induce someone to buy the asset. Thus, government bonds with low default risks pay lower interest rates than bonds of small companies with high default risks, even when figured on an after-tax basis. Likewise, stocks generally have to pay a higher return over the long haul, because the total return in any given time period is expected to fluctuate more. This is because stocks have a residual claim on company earnings, with stockholders being at the end of the claims line.

Some of the risks involved in investing can be greatly reduced by diversifying. The old saying, "Don't put all your eggs in one basket" captures the general idea. Investors reduce the percentage effect on their wealth of a bad turn of events by having more unrelated investments. Most of the risk reduction in stock holdings that occurs by holding unrelated stocks is achieved with a holding of fourteen stocks (Harrington, Fabozzi, and Fogler, 1990, p. 30). Such diversification protects against bad results because of fraud or mismanagement in a firm, bad results in a single industry, unfavorable weather, or other random events that do not have a pervasive market influence. There are some market-wide risks that cannot be diversified away. Such risks are called systematic risks, and are the only risks that should require a higher expected return to get people to be willing to hold securities. The reason is that diversifiable risk is easy to avoid and therefore should not require a premium.

Systematic risk may be related to a number of factors. For many years, the prevailing model in finance was the Capital Asset Pricing Model, which treated systematic risk of a stock as the degree to which the stock's return varied with the market. The definition of the market varied, but from a practical point of view was often taken to be the Standard & Poor's 500 stocks. In 1976, Stephen Ross developed the arbitrage pricing theory (APT), which challenged the idea of a single measure of systematic risk. According to Ross, arbitrage should result in the same risk premium applying at a moment in time for a particular factor. The factors in the U.S. economy that seem to give rise to risk premiums are related to industrial production, interest rates, and inflation (Chen, Roll, and Ross, 1986). Recent work has tended to support the APT as an explanation for differences in security returns (Harrington, Fabozzi, and Fogler, 1990, p. 21).

The APT maintains that, when all risk arbitrage profit opportunities have been eliminated, the expected return on a security is a linear function of its sensitivity to the risk factors that are priced in the market.

$E(R) = R_0 + B_1\ RP_1 + B_2\ RP_2 + \ldots + B_k\ RP_k$ (Solnik, 1988, p. 137). $E(R)$ is the expected return on the security. R_0 is the risk-free rate of return (usually taken to be the U.S. Treasury bill rate). RP_1 is the risk premium for factor 1. B_1 is the sensitivity to factor 1.

One can imagine a world of perfectly integrated financial markets that act to provide the foundation for investment in human and physical capital wherever the returns to such investment are the greatest. As economists, we sometimes assume such a framework for our analysis. Long-run efficiency in the allocation of resources over space and time does require such a role for financial capital. In such an integrated world, borrowing costs or the expected return would be the same for a given risk class, regardless of national or regional boundaries. However, the world in which we live may be quite different from the theoretical constructs of economic efficiency.

Given the relative disparities in human and physical capital per worker in the developed and developing world, an integrated global economy should move substantial capital resources to the less developed countries (LDCs). As Turner (1987) shows, however, such resource flows are but a small fraction of what would occur in a dynamically efficient world. Even among the developed countries, capital flows have been remarkably small. Paul Krugman (1989) suggests that Feldstein and Horioka (1980) were right, and we do not really have integrated capital markets.

Cho, Eun, and Senbet (1986) test and reject the joint hypothesis of the validity of the APT and an integrated global capital market. Their analysis indicates that some common factors are involved in movements in stock market returns in various countries. The pricing of the risk of the factors is not uniform. Their evidence indicates that risk premiums for common factors vary by country.

The implication of capital markets that are not fully integrated is that arbitrage opportunities are not fully exploited when expected risk factors are viewed globally. Most investors seem to prefer their own domestic habitat. They prefer to invest in their own country. In looking at Japanese investment, we should expect the Japanese to be willing to accept a lower return on the portion of their investments made in Japan for a given amount of risk. Some of this preference probably reflects the greater information costs of foreign investment, but regardless of why, the preference appears to exist.

JAPAN'S FOREIGN INVESTMENT

Japanese foreign investment has changed dramatically in the 1980s. The size and composition of Japanese investments have changed. The net Japanese position has changed because of macroeconomic forces in Japan and other countries, especially the United States. Changes in regulations in Japan have caused private sector capital flows to be more important in determining Japan's net capital position. Both assets and liabilities of Japan have grown as Japanese institutions and capital markets have become more integrated with global capital markets. Japanese foreign direct investment has also surged in the 1980s, and is important in many countries and industries.

The macroeconomic push to Japanese foreign investment came from Japan's slowing rate of growth and investment. Japanese savings remained high. The pull of the U.S. budget and trade deficits encouraged a

Japanese surplus. Consequently, the net foreign assets of Japan expanded from $11.5 billion in 1980 to $293.2 billion in 1989 (JEI Report No. 42A, 1989, p. 7; and *The Wall Street Journal,* May 29, 1990, p. A10). The 1989 figure is more than twenty-five times as large as in 1980. Japan's net asset position is sufficient to make it the world's largest creditor country. This distinction was held by the United States as recently as 1981 (JEI Report No. 42A, 1989, p. 1). The Reagan deficits have now resulted in the United States being the largest debtor country in the world. Further, even though the U.S. trade deficit is smaller, the United States continues to increase external debt by about $100 billion a year. Japan finances in total about half of this deficit.

Changes in regulations have made it easier for Japanese residents and institutions to invest in foreign countries. As a result, the net external position of the private sector went from $−16.7 billion in 1980 to $147.6 billion in 1988. The government net asset position went from $28.2 billion in 1980 to $144.2 billion in 1988. This represents an increase of more than five times for the Japanese government position. For Japanese private parties, it represents a reversal from being net debtors to the rest of the world to being large net creditors (JEI Report No. 42A, 1989, pp. 5–7).

Japanese external assets at the end of 1988 were $1,469.3 billion. External liabilities were $1,177.6 billion. Japanese external assets tend to be long-term (57%), and Japanese external liabilities tend to be short-term (73%). Consequently, Japanese net long-term assets were $521.0 billion, and Japanese net short-term assets were $−229.3 billion in 1988 (JEI Report No. 42A, 1989, p. 8).

Japanese private long-term investments were $728 billion in 1988. The majority, $427 billion or 59 percent, of these private assets were in securities such as stocks and bonds. Long-term trade credits were $49 billion (7%). Loans were $124 billion (17%). Japanese foreign direct investment was $111 billion, or 15 percent of private Japanese investment.

Nonofficial holdings of foreign assets as a percentage of Japanese portfolios were 7 percent in 1988. This is greater than the 2 percent of foreign assets held in U.S. portfolios, but less than the 15 percent in Germany or 22 percent in the United Kingdom. Japanese portfolio holdings of foreign securities have increased greatly since 1980 (Morgan Guaranty, 1989; JEI Report No. 42A, 1989).

Japanese Foreign Direct Investment by Country

Japanese foreign direct investment has greater impact than most other forms of investment. Direct investment includes real estate, plant and equipment directly owned by Japanese firms, and stock purchases greater than 10 percent in a company. These investments give Japanese investors decision-making powers, or at least the possibility of such powers, over foreign assets. Because of the possibility of such control, foreign nationals tends to get upset more about such investments than Japanese purchases of U.S. Treasury bonds.

Since countries are concerned about foreign direct investment, there is more detailed information about this type of investment than about portfolio investment in foreign securities. This section explores how Japan allocates its foreign direct investment. The approach is dynamic in the sense that the allocation decision is looked at over a fairly long time period (1965 to 1989). Some explanatory factors that are suggested by dynamic optimization of capital allocation are also studied.

As can be seen from table 8.1, Japan's foreign direct investment went from $949 million in 1965 to $186 billion in 1989. This represents an increase of 19,537 percent. U.S. inflation over this period was only 360 percent, so most of the increase in Japanese investment was real. Such investment represented 1 percent of Japanese gross national product (GNP) in 1965 and about 6 percent of Japanese GNP in 1989. If the earlier foreign direct investment is adjusted to 1988 dollars using a rough average of the inflation rate over the intervening years, Japanese total investment would be $3,400 (1965), $45,700 (1975), $142,500 (1985), and $249,900 (1989), in millions of 1988 dollars. This represents an increase of 7,250 percent. Clearly, major changes in the level of Japanese foreign investment have taken place in this twenty-four year period. Such a conservative adjustment assumes that the assets were able to earn enough locally to cover depreciation and inflation, but earned no real return.

Returning to the nominal figures, Japanese accumulated direct investment in the United States and Canada was 313 times greater in 1989 than in 1965. This increase is the largest dollar change ($74,851 million), as compared with Japan's investments in other countries. Western Europe experienced the largest percentage increase in Japanese investment, with the 1989 level at 1207 times the 1965 level. The Middle East had the smallest percentage increase. The 1989 level is "only" 17 times the 1965 level. Latin America includes offshore financial havens, and has the second lowest percentage increase (112 times the 1965 level).

The lower half of table 8.1 shows the shares of each region in Japan's total foreign direct investment in 1965, 1975, 1985, and 1989. A number of interesting patterns are revealed in this table. Significant changes occurred for Western Europe, Latin America, Oceania, and the Middle East between 1965 and 1975.

Europe's share of Japan's foreign direct investment increased five–fold, or a .13 share. Japanese direct investment in Europe was largely in finance, tourism-related agencies, and manufacturing. The manufacturing investment from the early 1970s was encouraged by the appreciation of the yen, which made production in Japan more costly, and by European pressures that encouraged manufacturing in Europe instead of

Table 8.1
Japanese Foreign Direct Investment by Region

	1965	1975	1985	March 1989
North America	$ 240	$3,917	$26,964	$75,091
Western Europe	25	2,518	11,002	30,164
Latin America & Offshore Havens	281	2,881	15,636	31,617
Asia	188	4,219	19,463	32,227
Oceania	8	930	4,243	9,315
Africa	11	501	3,370	4,604
Middle East	196	976	2,976	3,338
Total	949	15,943	83,648	186,356
(Shares of Each Region in Japan's Total for Each Year)				
North America	.25	.25	.32	.40
Western Europe	.03	.16	.13	.16
Latin America & Offshore Havens	.30	.18	.19	.17
Asia	.20	.26	.23	.17
Oceania	.01	.06	.05	.05
Africa	.01	.03	.04	.02
Middle East	.21	.06	.04	.02

Sources: 1965 and 1975 data are from the Japan Economic Research Center, Sekiguchi (1979); 1985 and 1989 data are from the Japan Economic Institute, JEI Report no. 39A, October 13, 1989.

Note: Cumulative balances in millions of then-current dollars.

exporting to European countries (Sekiguchi, 1982, pp. 167–68). Oceania also had a five-fold increase, to a .06 share.

Meanwhile, Latin America (primarily the financial havens) lost share. A decline of 40 percent, or a .12 share decline, occurred. The Middle East experienced a decline of .15 in the share of Japanese investment, from .21 to .06. This is a 71 percent decline in share. The U.S. share started at .25 in 1965, increased in 1985, and increased further by 1989 to .40. This is a 60 percent increase in share over this period.

Table 8.2 provides information on regional shares in 1985 of (1) Japanese foreign direct investment, (2) World GNP of the market economies excluding Japan, (3) World population excluding Japan, (4) Japan's exports, (5) Japan's imports, and (6) Japan's total trade. Variables 2–6 are seen as possible explanations for Japan's global investment pattern.

The diversification motive should lead to Japanese investment that is roughly proportional to the distribution of wealth. GNP is taken as a proxy for wealth. This motivation does seem to be important to Japanese investors. Allocational efficiency of capital would cause capital to flow to where it would do the most good (have the highest social return). People are the prime users and potential beneficiaries of capital. If this motivation holds, then Japanese capital should be distributed roughly proportionally to population. This does not seem to occur. Japanese investment could also be tied to extractive or distributional needs of Japanese importers and exporters. If so, Japanese investment should be roughly proportional to Japanese imports, exports, or total trade. There does appear to be some such connection between Japanese trade and investment.

A passive investment pattern would essentially follow an index of global investments. At least foreign investment would be proportional to foreign market valuation, even if domestic investors overweighted their portfolios in favor of domestic assets. Since market valuations are not readily available for all the regions, I have used GNP as a proxy for capital values. Of course, GNP is not always consistent with market values. A notable case is Japan itself, which has a much higher share of world market valuation than it does of world GNP. Nevertheless, the assumption is that a desire to diversify foreign holdings will lead Japanese investors to have investment shares in regions that are roughly equal to their share in non-Japanese GNP.

Looking at tables 8.1 and 8.2, we see that this explanation of Japanese investment has considerable explanatory power. North America in all periods has received the most Japanese foreign direct investment, and it is the region with the greatest share of GNP. Further, the recent liberalization of Japanese financial markets and institutions in the 1980s (see Feldman, 1986) seems to have increased this tendency. The North American share rose to .32 in 1985, and to .40 in 1989. This brings the North American share of Japanese investment closer to the .45 share of North America in non-Japanese global GNP.

The Spearman rank correlation of Japan's foreign direct investment share and world GNP share is .75. The Spearman rank correlation is designed to show whether ranking entities by one variable is related to ranking the entities by another variable (Guilford and Fruchter, 1973, pp. 283–85). An example would be to rank people by education and by income. If people highly ranked by education were also highly ranked by

Table 8.2
Japanese Foreign Direct Investment, 1985 Share Analysis

	Japan's Foreign Direct Investment	World GNP[a]	World[b] Population	Japan's Exports	Japan's Imports	Japan's Total Trade
North America	.32	.45	.06	.40	.24	.33
Western Europe	.13	.30	.10	.14	.10	.12
Latin America & Offshore Havens	.19	.08	.09	.05	.05	.05
Asia	.23	.10	.57	.26	.28	.27
Oceania	.05	.02	.01	.04	.06	.05
Africa	.04	.04	.12	.04	.05	.05
Middle East	.04	.05	.02	.05	.20	.11
Spearman's Rank Correlation of shares with Japan's Foreign Investment		.75	.29	.68	.39	.64

(.71 is significant at the .05 level for a one-tailed test)

Sources: United Nations, *Yearbook of National Accounts Statistics, 1985* and *Yearbook of International Trade Statistics, 1985.*

[a] Excluding Japan and the centrally planned economies except China.
[b] Excluding Japan.

income, then a positive relationship would exist between education and income. Further work could then explore just how education and income were interrelated. The .75 Spearman rank correlation indicates a positive relationship at the .05 level of significance. In other words, there is less than a 5 percent chance that no relationship really exists between Japanese investment share and GNP share of a country.

An alternative theory of investment would be for the flow of capital to seek the highest social return. In a perfect world, this would also be the highest private return. This would result in financial flows to those countries most in need of human and physical capital. This would tend to draw capital toward population areas with relatively little endogenous capital. I used the share of world population as a proxy for this variable. As can be seen in table 8.2, the share of population does not do a good job of explaining the pattern of Japanese investments. The Spearman rank correlation coefficient between the shares of Japanese foreign investment and world population is .29, which is very weak.

The last three variables relate to Japanese foreign trade. They are the share of Japanese imports, exports, and total trade. It is quite possible that Japanese exporters and importers buy or develop facilities in various countries in furtherance of trade activities. It appears that, of the trade-related measures, Japanese exports are most closely related to investment. The Spearman rank correlation coefficient for export shares and investment shares is .68, which is slightly below the .05 level of significance.

It appears that Japan has acted basically as an investor seeking to diversify international holdings. There has not been a noticeable push in the direction of investing for the long-run development of LDCs. We do not yet have an integrated global economy in the sense of providing capital resources where they are most needed for economic development. Japanese trading patterns appear to have an effect on Japanese foreign direct investment patterns.

Japanese Foreign Direct Investment by Industry

There have been major changes in the pattern of Japanese foreign direct investment in the last twenty-five years, as shown in table 8.3. Japanese direct investment in the 1960s and 1970s was almost equally weighted between manufacturing, mining, and other investment areas (real estate and services). By the end of the 1980s, services and real estate came to dominate Japanese direct investments, accounting for 65 percent of the total. Manufacturing had fallen to about a fourth of the total (27%). Mining was only 7 percent of total Japanese direct investment by 1989.

Japanese foreign direct investment in the "other" category has shown tremendous growth since 1965. This category includes such industries as trade and sales; banking, finance, and insurance; real estate; construction; transportation; services; and others. The most important of these in 1989 are listed in table 8.3 as subcategories under "other" for 1985 and 1989.

These "other" industries represent what are sometimes called tertiary industries or the service sector. Primary industries are mining, agriculture, and fisheries. Secondary industries are manufacturing industries, especially basic industries like chemicals and metals. Japanese foreign direct investment patterns reveal the much greater growth abroad of Japan's tertiary economic sector in the last twenty years. I shall refer to "other" as the service sector of the economy for ease of discussion.

The service sector had $281 million of Japanese foreign direct invest-

Table 8.3
Japanese Foreign Direct Investment by Industry

	1965	1975	1985	March 1989
Manufacturing	$ 337	$ 5,164	$24,400	$ 49,843
	(.36)	(.32)	(.29)	(.27)
Chemicals			$ 3,982	$ 6,540
Metals			$ 5,190	$ 7,671
Electric Machinery			$ 3,747	$ 10,196
Transport Equipment			$ 1,842	$ 7,031
Other Manufacturing			$ 9,639	$ 18,405
Agriculture & Forestry	$ 15	$ 215	$ 780	$ 1,054
	(.02)	(.01)	(.01)	(.01)
Fisheries	$ 8	$ 130	$ 442	$ 632
	(.01)	(.01)	(.01)	(.003)
Mining	$ 308	$ 4,131	$11,756	$ 13,949
	(.32)	(.26)	(.14)	(.07)
Other Industries	$ 281	$ 6,302	$46,272	$120,878
	(.30)	(.40)	(.55)	(.65)
Trade & Sales			$12,677	$ 20,011
Banking, Finance, & Insurance			$10,859	$ 41,876
Real Estate			$ 2,533	$ 20,599
TOTAL	$ 949	$15,943	$83,650	$186,356

Sources: 1965 and 1975 data are from the Japan Economic Research Center, Sekiguchi (1979); 1985 and 1989 data are from the Japan Economic Institute, JEI Report no. 39A, October 13, 1989.

Notes: Cumulative balances in millions of then-current dollars. Figures in parentheses indicate shares of each industry in Japan's total foreign direct investment.

ment in 1965. This increased more than twenty-fold to $6.3 billion in 1975; there was more than a seven-fold increase from 1975 to 1985. Direct foreign investments in services more than doubled between 1985 and 1989, to $120.9 billion. The 1989 level of Japanese foreign direct investment was more than 430 times the level in 1965. Dollar prices during this time rose about 3.6 times. This means that even if the accumulated investment were deflated by 3.6, the real increase in foreign direct investment in the service sector would be about 120-fold from 1965 to 1989. During this same period of time, Japanese investment in fixed capital in their domestic economy increased about ten times. In the United States, by contrast, real investment only increased about 1.5 times from 1965 to 1989.

Real estate was the fastest-growing service sector for Japanese foreign direct investment from 1985 to 1989. Japanese foreign real estate investments went from $2.5 billion to $20.6 billion. This is more than a sevenfold increase. By 1989, real estate was the second-largest industry for Japanese direct investment.

Japanese foreign direct investment in banking, finance, and insurance increased more than 2.5 times from 1985 to 1986. Investment in this sector went from $10.9 billion to $41.9 billion. In 1989, banking, finance, and insurance had more Japanese foreign investment than any other industry.

Japanese foreign direct investment in trade and sales "only" grew about 60 percent from 1985 to 1989. At the end of the period, it was the third-largest industry for Japanese direct investment instead of the largest as it was in 1985. The increase was from $12.7 billion in 1985 to $20.0 billion in 1989.

Japanese foreign direct investment in manufacturing has increased substantially since 1965. The rate of growth (a 147-fold increase) has been lower than for investment in services (a 429-fold increase). The result is that manufacturing accounts for a lower share of Japanese total foreign direct investment in 1989 (27%) than it did in 1965 (36%). Nevertheless, Japanese foreign direct investment in manufacturing has more than doubled since 1985.

The fastest-growing area of Japanese foreign direct investment in manufacturing is in transport equipment for the 1985 to 1989 period. Direct investment in transport equipment increased from $1.8 billion in 1985 to $7.0 billion in 1989. This is an increase of 282 percent. Japanese direct investment in electric machinery manufacturing went from $3.7 billion in 1985 to $10.2 billion in 1989, an increase of 172 percent. The next-fastest growth category for Japanese foreign direct investment in manufacturing was the catchall category of "other manufacturing," which increased 91 percent from 1985 to 1989.

Japanese direct foreign investment in mining has declined in relative importance since 1965. In 1965, mining investment was 32 percent of all Japanese foreign direct investment. The percentage of mining fell to 26 percent in 1975, to 14 percent in 1985, and to 7 percent in 1989. Actual investment in mining increased throughout this period, but at a much slower rate than services or manufacturing. The level of Japanese direct investment in mining was $13.9 billion in 1989, which was forty-five times as great as the $.3 billion in 1965. This represents an increase in real terms of more than twelve times, which is not substantially faster than Japanese domestic investment.

SUMMARY

Japanese investment in Japan's domestic economy has grown rapidly over the last few decades, but Japanese foreign investment has grown even faster. There have been a number of liberalizations of controls on Japanese capital flows in the 1970s and 1980s. Japan's reduced investment options at home as its economy matured have also played a role. Japan's capital outflow to the rest of the world has raised it to the rank of the world's largest creditor nation.

Japanese foreign direct investment is distributed across many countries, with the larger GNP countries getting more. It also appears that more Japanese investment goes to countries with more trade with Japan. Regions with greater populations do not seem to receive more Japanese investment unless they also have more GNP. Consequently, Japan's investors have not significantly overcome the reluctance of private investors to allocate capital to LDCs.

Japanese foreign direct investment has increased most rapidly in the service sector, where it is now more than 430 times its level in 1965. Banking, finance, and insurance had the greatest amount of Japanese foreign direct investment in 1989, with $41.9 billion. Japanese foreign direct investment in manufacturing has grown 147-fold since 1965, but this has resulted in a decrease in its share of total Japanese foreign direct investment to 27 percent, because of services' rapid increase. Japanese foreign direct investment in mining has increased since 1965, but only slightly faster than Japanese domestic investment. Consequently, mining's share of Japanese foreign direct investment has fallen from 32 percent in 1965 to 7 percent in 1989.

9 Foreign Investment in Japan

Residents of other countries desire investments in Japan to earn a higher expected return or to lower their investment risk. A passive global portfolio would include substantial Japanese assets. Protection against exchange rate changes could motivate firms that export to or import from Japan. Some firms may invest in Japan for specific locational reasons such as establishing a Japanese distributional network.

During the rapid growth phase in Japan, capital investment within Japan could be expected to earn a higher real return than in the United States or other "mature" economies. Economic growth theory predicts declining marginal product of capital as additional capital is added to a given work force (Solow, 1970). As we saw in table 1.1, Japan had a much lower stock of capital per worker in the 1950s and 1960s than the United States did. Recently, however, the situation has been reversed. So, in the earlier period, the pursuit of a higher rate of return might have lured financial capital to Japan even if the perceived risk were higher. At the present time, the real return over an extended period is likely to be lower in Japan than elsewhere. Consequently, it is likely that risk reduction will be the dominant motive for most long-run investors in Japan.

Long-run investors are singled out for this part of basic economic analysis because all economies go through cycles. Someone who is able to correctly predict the economic cycle of Japan could make money through such cyclical investment. Many have tried to predict such cycles and failed to make money (Gibson, 1990, pp. 69–77). However, some investment will be taking place in Japan at any given time, as a bet that the

Japanese market will rise faster than the rest of the world's, regardless of fundamental economic relationships.

If the global capital market were fully integrated, investors in any country would expect approximately the same return for investments of similar sensitivity to the factors that caused systematic changes in asset prices. As noted in chapter 8, researchers have found that global markets are not integrated to that extent (Cho, Eun, and Senbet, 1986). Given that the global market is not fully integrated, then the preference of individual and institutional investors will play a role in determining expected relative returns.

The Japanese seem to prefer investment in Japan to investment overseas. Since the Japanese are making overseas investments on a fairly large scale, this would indicate that the expected return in Japan is lower than in the rest of the world. Nevertheless, since Japan is a large capital market, there will also be a large investment by foreigners in Japan.

A principal means of reducing risk is to hold a diversified portfolio of assets. If two asset values do not move in concert then, by holding both, an investor reduces the expected variability of her portfolio. If two asset returns are negatively related (negative covariance), holding both reduces portfolio variability even more.

Solnik (1988, pp. 46–47) has found that international diversification can reduce portfolio risk by 50 percent. Basically, securities from different countries are less correlated than securities within the countries. Stock prices in Japan and the Untied States can move in different directions. The correlation between the U.S. stock market and Japan's over the 1971 to 1986 period was just .27. Japan's stock market and West Germany's had a .45 correlation. Japan and the world index of stock returns had a .60 correlation (Solnik, 1988, pp. 40–41).

At the end of 1987, the total market value of Japan's stock market was greater than that of any other country. It represented 42 percent of the total world market value. The U.S. market had the second-highest value, at 31 percent of total world market value (Honeygold, 1989, p. 55).

Japan's market continued to have a higher valuation than the U.S. market at the beginning of the 1990s. By the fall of 1990, there has been a 45 percent fall in yen values of Japan's stocks. This has reversed the relative market valuation of U.S. and Japanese stocks. Nevertheless, Japan's stock market valuation remains one of the largest in the world.

Any prudent investor would hold significant shares of Japanese stocks in a globally diversified portfolio. A passive investment policy would hold shares equal to the market value of Japan in the world portfolio. An active policy would differ from a world market portfolio based on the portfolio manager's expectations regarding various markets and foreign exchange rates (Solnik, 1988, p. 345).

Some companies may invest in Japan as a hedge against other activities that expose them to Japanese foreign exchange or market risk. A capital goods producer in the United States might choose to invest in Japanese machine tool makers so that when his competitors were favored by exchange rate changes, his losses were reduced by gains in Japan. Of course, such activity is limited by various anti-trust laws. Also, it is possible for market changes to reduce all capital goods producers' profits regardless of country. A more general investment in Japanese stocks might protect against both of these risks while avoiding antitrust problems. Some direct foreign investment in Japan is also likely as a hedging strategy.

Foreign investment in Japan was $1,177 billion at the end of 1988. Most of this investment is in the form of short-term liquid assets ($865 billion). Long-term investment of $312 billion is only 27 percent of the total. Most (81%) of the long-term investment is investment in Japanese securities. Foreign direct investment at the end of 1988 was only $10.4 billion, or 3.3 percent of long-term foreign investment in Japan (JEI Report No. 42A, 1989, p. 8).

FOREIGN DIRECT INVESTMENT IN JAPAN

Foreign direct investment in Japan has risen dramatically over the last thirty-three years. The United States has the most direct investment in Japan. Most direct investment in Japan is in manufacturing industries.

As shown in table 9.1 total foreign direct investment in Japan in 1988 was $10.4 billion. This is 361 times the level of foreign direct investment in Japan in 1955. Still, it is only 9.4 percent as large as the $110.8 billion of foreign direct investment by Japan at the end of 1988 (JEI Report No. 42A, 1989, p. 9).

The level of foreign direct investment in Japan was $272 million in 1965, or 9.4 times the level of $28.8 million in 1955. In 1974, direct investment in Japan was $1.2 billion, 4.3 times the level in 1965. In 1985, foreign direct investment in Japan had risen to $6.7 billion, which is 5.7 times the level in 1974.

Of course, much of the increase between 1974 and 1985 is inflationary, since dollar prices almost doubled over this period. Prices from 1965 to 1974 went up about 70 percent. Prices from 1955 to 1965 increased "only" about 25 percent.

It is not clear how to adjust investment figures for inflation. Unlike flow items like the gross national product (GNP), direct investments take the form of long-lived assets whose replacement costs increase with inflation. Thus, earlier investments are accumulated at original costs, which understates the present level of direct investment. This would tend to cause the calculated growth in investment to understate the real growth

Table 9.1
Foreign Direct Investment in Japan by Region of Origin

	1955	1965	1974	1985	1988[b]
United States	$20.4	$189.7	$821.0	$3,495.0	$5,520.0
Canada	2.1	7.6	34.4	124.0	208.0
United Kingdom	4.3	21.2	86.2	360.0	521.0
West Germany	.9	3.3	45.3	238.0	417.0
Switzerland	0	24.1	75.9	335.0	521.0
Other Western Europe	.5	6.4	54.3	304.0[a]	521.0
Others	.6	19.7	47.7	1,797.0	2,812.0
Total	$28.8	$272.0	$1,164.8	$6,653.0	$10,416.0
	(Shares of Each Region in Japan's Total for Each Year)				
United States	.71	.70	.70	.53	
Canada	.07	.03	.03	.02	
United Kingdom	.15	.08	.07	.05	
West Germany	.03	.01	.04	.04	
Switzerland	NA	.09	.07	.05	
Other Western Europe	.02	.02	.05	.05	
Others	.02	.07	.04	.27	

Sources: 1955–74 data are from Keizai Chosa Kyokai, *Direct Foreign Investment in Japan 1976,* cited in Sekiguchi (1979); 1985 data are from *Japan 1986: An International Comparison,* 1986, cited in Higashi and Lauter (1987); 1988 data are from Japan Economic Institute, JEI Report no. 42A, November 3, 1989.

Note: Cumulative balances in millions of then-current dollars.
[a] Only includes other Western European countries listed by name in Higashi and Lauter, 1987.
[b] Country figures are estimated as 1985 shares times 1988 total foreign direct investment in Japan.

in Japan. By the same token, the higher prices paid in the later periods tend to exaggerate the rate of increase in investment.

The investment figures have been left in current dollar terms because of the problems of revaluing investment every year. If adjustment were made for dollar price changes, the increases for the periods would be lower. The 1965 level would be 7.6 times the 1955 level, the 1974 level would be 2.6 times the 1965 level, and the 1985 level would be 2.9 times the 1974 level. The 1989 level would be 81 times that in 1955, instead of 361. The increases in real investment levels should be somewhere between the rates calculated with nominal values and the rate of increases shown here.

Foreign Direct Investment in Japan by Country of Origin

The United States has been the dominant investing country in Japan. In 1955, the United States had $20.4 million in direct investments in Japan. This was 71 percent of the total foreign direct investment in Japan as of that year. The U.S. share of the GNP of the market economies excluding Japan was .47 in 1955. So U.S. total foreign direct investment in Japan was considerably greater than what would be expected based on U.S. relative income.

The U.S. share of foreign direct investment in Japan stayed at about 70 percent in 1965 and 1975. In 1985, the U.S. share had fallen to 53 percent of total foreign direct investment in Japan. The U.S. share of non-Japanese GNP fell to .34 in 1975, and then increased to .41 in 1985. As discussed earlier, U.S. GNP is overstated by using market exchange rates in 1985. The dollar was overvalued, which leads to unrealistically high comparative income. Even at the end of the period considered here, the United States had more direct investment in Japan than the U.S. income share would predict.

Other countries with major direct investments in Japan include the United Kingdom, Switzerland, West Germany, and Canada. In 1955, the United Kingdom had 15 percent of the foreign direct investment in Japan. This compares to the United Kingdom's 6 percent share of non-Japanese GNP. The United Kingdom's share of direct investment in Japan fell over the period shown in table 9.1 to 5 percent in 1985. The United Kingdom's share of non-Japanese GNP had also declined to about 5 percent by 1985.

Canada had 7 percent of foreign direct investment in Japan in 1955, compared to 4 percent of non-Japanese GNP. Canada's share dropped to 2 percent of total direct investment in Japan by 1985. Canada's share of non-Japanese GNP was still approximately 4 percent in 1985. Canada's investment share in Japan goes from a position of being greater than its GNP share to being less than its GNP share. Canada exported to Japan about 4 percent of Japan's imports throughout the postwar period.

Switzerland had no appreciable investment in Japan in 1955. Its share of foreign direct investment peaked at 9 percent in 1965. Switzerland's share of direct investment declined to 5 percent by 1985.

West Germany had 3 percent of direct investment in Japan in 1955. This fell to 1 percent in 1965, and then rose to 4 percent in 1975 and 1985. West Germany's share of GNP in the market economies outside of Japan ranged from 6 percent in 1955 to 9 percent in 1975. West Germany's foreign direct investment in Japan was always less over this period than its share of GNP.

The United States is the only country listed that consistently had direct investments in Japan that were greater than its income share in the global market economy (excluding Japan). The United Kingdom and Canada invested more than their income shares early in the period, but not late in the period. Switzerland invested more than its income share from 1965 to 1985. West Germany never invested as much as its proportional income share. In 1985, other countries together held 27 percent of total direct foreign investment in Japan.

Foreign Direct Investment in Japan by Industry

Throughout the postwar period, foreign direct investment in Japan has predominantly been in manufacturing industries. Over time, the importance of direct investment in commerce (wholesale and retail) has become more important. Real estate holdings are more important now than thirty years ago, but remain a fairly small portion of total foreign direct investment in Japan.

Foreign direct investment in Japanese manufacturing has gone from $26.8 million in 1955 to $7.0 billion in 1988, as shown in table 9.2. The 1988 level is 261 times the 1955 level. If 1955 investment is converted to 1988 dollar prices, then the 1988 level is 58 times the 1955 level. This is a more rapid rate of increase than the level of Japanese investment as a whole.

Foreign direct investment in manufacturing was 93 percent of total foreign direct investment in Japan in 1955. This share increased to 94 percent in 1965, and then fell. It was down to 83 percent in 1974, and an estimated 67 percent in 1988.

Foreign direct investment in petroleum was the largest sector of foreign investment in manufacturing in 1955 and 1965. By 1975, there was more foreign direct investment in the Japanese machinery industry. Petroleum investment again rose to the fore in 1985, based on U.S. foreign direct investment. Petroleum and machinery were equal in foreign direct investment by 1988. The Japanese chemical industry has also been the recipient of substantial foreign direct investment, with $1.5 billion by 1988.

Table 9.2
Foreign Direct Investment in Japan by Industry

	1955	1965	1974	1985[a]	1988[a]
Manufacturing	$26.8	$256.4	$1,105.3	$4,900.0	$7,000.0
Chemicals	4.6	67.7	260.8	900.0	1,500.0
Petroleum	14.1	89.1	223.8	1,600.0	2,200.0
Machinery	4.0	61.5	259.4	1,500.0	2,200.0
Other Manufacturing	4.1	38.1	361.3	900.0	1,200.0
Real Estate	.1	.4	3.1	400.0	700.0
Transportation & Communications	.2	.5	10.6	NA	NA
Commerce (Trade & Sales)	1.6	6.1	125.8	1,100.0	2,200.0
Others	.1	8.7	88.2	300.0	500.0
TOTAL	$28.8	$272.1	$1,333.0	$6,653.0	$10,416.0
(Shares of Each Industry in Foreign Direct Investment in Japan)					
Manufacturing	.93	.94	.83	.73	.67
Real Estate	.003	.001	.002	.06	.07
Transportation & Communications	.007	.002	.008	NA	NA
Commerce	.06	.02	.09	.17	.21
Others	.003	.03	.07	.04	.05

Sources: 1955–74 data are from Keizai Chosa Kyokai, *Direct Foreign Investment in Japan 1976,* cited in Sekiguchi (1979).

Note: Cumulative balances in millions of then-current dollars.

[a] 1985 and 1988 data are estimated as having the same industry shares as United States foreign direct investment in Japan, as per Japan Economic Institute, JEI Report no. 39A, October 13, 1989, p. 45. The totals for 1985 and 1988 are the same as in Table 9.1.

Foreign direct investment in Japan's commerce, mostly wholesale trade, has gone from $1.6 million in 1955 to $2.2 billion in 1988. This is an increase of 1,374 times. Adjusted for price changes, the increase is still 306 times the 1955 level. The amount directly invested in commerce has doubled since 1985.

Foreign direct investment in real estate is 7,000 times the level in 1955. This is 225 times as high as the $3.1 million in 1974. Virtually all of the direct investment in Japanese real estate has come in the 1980s. This reflects the changes in Japanese laws and regulations that in 1980 began to treat foreign investment as "free in principle" instead of restricted (Higashi and Lauter, 1987, p. 159).

Foreign direct investment in Japan has grown dramatically over the years. It is, however, still but a small part of total foreign investment in Japan. Foreign direct investment in 1988 was only .8 of a percent of total foreign investment in Japan. That is, all other forms of foreign investment in Japan were 112 times as large as foreign direct investment in Japan. Short-term liquid investment in Japan was eighty-three times as large as foreign direct investment. Foreign portfolio investment in Japanese securities were twenty-four times as large as foreign direct investment in Japan.

Part of the small relative size of foreign direct investment in Japan has to do with the relative attractiveness of other investments. On Japan's side of the ledger, total foreign investment by Japan in other types of investments is twelve times the level of Japanese foreign direct investment. Japanese investment in foreign securities is four times the level of Japanese foreign direct investment.

Japanese foreign direct investment abroad is relatively greater than foreign direct investment in Japan. Consequently, at the end of 1988, Japanese assets abroad were only 25 percent higher than Japanese liabilities, for a total net credit position of $291 billion. Japanese foreign direct investment abroad was 963 percent higher than foreign direct investment in Japan, for a net difference of $100 billion. Most of this difference has occurred since the dollar peaked in February, 1985. With the strength of the Japanese yen, the Japanese have sharply increased their foreign direct investments.

SUMMARY

Foreign investment in Japan is large, but Japan's economy is so large that foreign investment is only a small percentage of total investment in Japanese assets. Much of the incentive for investment in Japan today is for diversification. On fundamentals like earnings and dividend yields, Japanese stocks are still not particularly attractive by global standards, even after they have declined in value by more than 40 percent. Nevertheless, Japan's stock market still accounts for a major portion of the world's market value. Global portfolios will need significant amounts of Japanese stocks.

Foreign direct investment in Japan has grown at a rapid rate over the last twenty years. The overall level of such investment, however, remains modest. It is small relative to total investment in Japan and relative to Japanese foreign direct investment abroad. Investment in manufacturing facilities in Japan is not as big a part of foreign direct investment in Japan as it was earlier. Direct investment in plant and equipment or in a whole company should increase when it is undervalued relative to the rest of the world. This is surely not the case for Japan at the present time.

10 JAPAN AND THE UNITED STATES

Japan and the United States are the most economically powerful countries in the world. Together with the soon-to-be-unified Europe (European Economic Community [EEC]), they determine to a large extent the state of the global economy. The relationship between Japan and the United States has been extremely important to Japan's economic well-being over the entire postwar period. With Japan's rapid economic growth and high savings rate, the economic well-being of the United States has become increasingly dependent upon its relationship with Japan.

Citizens, workers, businesspeople, and policymakers of both countries need to understand how the two countries are linked together to be better able to promote mutually beneficial economic advantages. The countries also have differences that will sometimes put them on opposite sides of an issue. Allies and friends do not always have to view issues from the same perspective. Respect for each other's views will be furthered by a greater understanding of the economic relationship between the two countries.

The United States has been the dominant country in the global economy since the end of the Second World War. Japan's rise to be the second-largest market economy and its continued growth worry U.S. residents. The fact that the United States and Japan compete with each other in a number of export markets heightens the tension felt in the United States when Japan succeeds.

Japan and the United States are important to each other as export markets and as providers of import goods. Both countries have used tariff and nontariff barriers in the past against the other's products and both continue to do so today. Both countries are dependent upon imported oil, with Japan's dependence being virtually 100 percent.

The United States and Japan have both pursued active macroeconomic policies in the postwar period. The goals of these policies have been the achievement of (1) low unemployment, (2) low inflation, (3) controllable budget and trade balances, and (4) sustained economic growth. Most analysts are likely to conclude that Japan has been and continues to be more successful at achieving most of these macroeconomic objectives.

The United States and Japan are important to each other and the rest of the world as investment markets and sources. The United States is both the largest investor in Japan and the largest investment market for the Japanese. Japan and the United States both have a major presence in the capital markets of other countries. The United States and Japan are also the largest contributors of official development assistance.

With cooperation between the United States and Japan, major issues facing the global economy can be resolved in positive ways. Trade barriers can be eased. Capital flows can be freed to further sustain economic development in capital-short less developed countries (LDCs). Most economies can come to count on relatively stable exchange rates and lowered barriers to trade, which will further the global integration of markets. Unemployment and inflation can be reduced in the global economy with reasonable coordinated policies. Without cooperation, these objectives cannot hope to be accomplished.

INCOME

Relative income is of great importance to people. Relative income also affects nations. The United States has been in a relative decline in the global market throughout the post-World War II period, with the exception of the 1980–85 surge in reported income due to the surge in the value of the dollar. Japan, on the other hand, has had its relative income steadily increase over the postwar period, and it continues to do so. It is this change in relative income that has tended to upset Americans.

The decline in the relative income of the United States was almost inevitable because of how high it actually was following World War II. In 1955, the U.S. gross national product (GNP) was 46 percent of the total GNP of all the market-oriented economies in the world. In other words, out of every $100 of goods produced in the market economies (those outside the Soviet Bloc), $46 of them were produced in the United States. This was true in spite of the fact that the United States had only 6 percent of the world's population. The United States also consumed a lion's share of the world's goods. By 1985, the U.S. share of global GNP (market economies) was 36 percent, and its population was only 5 percent of global population. This still leaves the U.S. share much higher than its population share, but not by as large a margin. These figures come from United Nations *World Population Prospects* (1989) and *Yearbook of National Accounts Statistics.* The GNP figures are calculated by translating national currency figures into dollars using market exchange rates.

The procedure of translating national accounts by exchange rates has its drawbacks. The major problem is that there are differences in relative prices in various countries. Goods that are freely traded and have low transportation costs would tend to cost about the same translated by exchange rates wherever they were consumed. Other goods, like housing and personal services, tend to be much more expensive relative to traded goods in some countries than in others. Also, goods that are protected in a country, like rice in Japan, will tend to be much more expensive in that country than in the global market. These and other considerations have led a number of researchers to adjust the national accounts to equivalent purchasing power. They have essentially improved the measure of what goods and services can be purchased with the GNP of various countries (Kravis, et al., 1975). Somewhat later, I will present such an analysis of relative real income between the United States and Japan, real in the sense of what real goods and services can be purchased with the stated income. When income comparisons are made in terms of real purchasing power, the U.S. relative position is enhanced over comparisons using exchange rates.

Such a refined measure of relative income gives a better idea of changes in people's welfare (satisfaction). On the other hand, comparisons between countries based on market exchange rates have some merits as well. When we are examining how important a market is for the global economy, we want to know what potential purchases could take place. It is not just the current pattern of purchases and prices that are important, but also potential purchases. It is current income evaluated at current market exchange rates that tells us this information.

Perhaps an intracountry regional example will help make the point. In 1985, per capita income in New York City was $11,188. Per capita income in Norfolk, Virginia, was $9,340 (U.S. Bureau of the Census, *County and City Data Book,* 1988). There is no need to translate by means of an exchange rate, since both areas use dollars as their currency. The apparent result is that income was higher in New York than it was in Norfolk. However, if we adjust for different costs of living, the result changes.

New York City has higher living costs than Norfolk. According to the *Cost of Living Index* compiled by the American Chamber of Commerce Researchers Association, it cost $136.30 in New York to buy what cost $101.10 to buy in Norfolk. A big part of the difference was higher housing costs. Adjusted for these differences, New York City real purchasing power per capita income was only 89 percent of what it was in Norfolk in 1985.

One reason for exploring changes in income and in wealth with the market exchange rate translation is the fragile nature of such a translation. Understanding how exchange rates change perceived wealth and income facilitates an understanding of international linkages. When the Japanese yen appreciates in value, Japanese income translated to dollars at the going exchange rate would be able to buy more goods from the United States or other countries pricing their goods in dollars. On the other hand, if a significant number of the Japanese start buying such goods, the demand for the dollar increases and the yen will be depreciated. It is almost a "catch-22" situation. Japanese income and wealth are high at a high value of the yen, but much of the translated wealth and income disappears if the Japanese seek to buy the world's goods or assets at too rapid a rate.

Of course, the same relationship between a country's currency and its purchasing power exists for other countries. One requirement of a global stabilization policy is to determine what stable exchange rates are appropriate for various countries. The policies to maintain such exchange rates can take many forms, but they need to be able to respond to a number of changes.

With data reported in the *International Financial Statistics* of the International Monetary Fund (1990), we can make some simple calculations to show the fluctuations in relative income between the United States and Japan. In the last quarter of 1989, Japan's annualized GNP level was 401.4 trillion yen. The United States annualized GNP for the fourth quarter of 1989 was $5.3 trillion. The yen/dollar exchange rate at the end of 1989 was 143 yen/dollar. Japan's GNP converted at this rate was $2.8 trillion, 401.4 trillion yen ÷ 143 = $2.8 trillion. At the end of 1989, Japanese GNP was 53 percent as large as that of the United States using current exchange rates, $2.8 trillion ÷ $5.3 trillion = .53. In 1989, Japan's population was 123 million and the U.S. population was 249 million. Thus, U.S. per capita income at the end of 1989 was $21,285, $5.3 trillion ÷ 249 million = $21,285. Japan's per capita GNP was 3,263,780 yen, 401.4 trillion yen ÷ 123 million = 3,263,780 yen. Converting this per capita income at the exchange rate of 143 yen/dollar yields Japanese per capita income of $22,824 at the end of 1989. Using this translation of Japanese income results in the estimate that Japanese income per capita was 107 percent of U.S. per capita income at the end of 1989. Consequently, if Japanese income were spent on internationally traded goods or assets, the average Japanese could have bought 7 percent more than the average U.S. citizen at the end of 1989.

Similar calculations could be performed to translate Japanese income into dollars at different exchange rates. As of fall 1990, the Japanese exchange rate is about 140 yen/dollar. At this rate, Japan's income at the end of 1989 would be $2.9 trillion, or 54 percent of the U.S. level. Japanese per capita GNP in dollars would be $23,577, or 111 percent of U.S. per capita income. As the yen appreciates further, Japanese global purchasing power increases.

In April 1990, the exchange rate was 158 yen/dollar. This rate would show Japanese GNP as 48 percent of the U.S. level. Japanese per capita income translated at 158 yen/dollar would be 97 percent of the U.S. per capita income level. On the other hand, the 1988 exchange rate was 124 yen/dollar. If Japanese GNP at the end of 1989 were translated at the 1988 rate, it would be 61 percent of the U.S. GNP. Japanese per capita income would be 124 percent of U.S. per capita income at 124 yen/dollar.

Clearly, there have been major fluctuations in exchange rates, even after the Plaza and Louvre accords, where the countries of the Group of Seven declared their intention to stabilize exchange rates. There is no magic exchange rate that will bring about full employment, low inflation, and steady economic growth. In fact, any given exchange rate could be accomplished with changes in money supplies, prices, and other factors. It appears that a convergence to 140 yen/dollar or thereabouts is certainly possible, given the fluctuations of the last few years. That is approximately the present exchange rate, and at that level, Japanese per capita income would be 11 percent higher than the U.S. level.

Using current exchange rates to translate GNP, the Japanese accomplishment of high sustained growth can be appreciated. In table 1.1, GNP per worker is reported for Japan and the United States. Since the people per worker ratio is similar in the two countries, the ratio of GNP per capita is about the same as GNP per worker. Using this relationship, we see that Japanese GNP per capita was 10 percent of the U.S. level in 1955. It increased to 21 percent in 1965, 57 percent in 1975, 65 percent in 1985, and 107 percent in 1989. By 1995, Japanese GNP per capita might well be 137 percent of the U.S. level as shown in table 1.1.

This remarkable growth in income in Japan is to some extent an illustration of the power of compound interest. The Japanese have saved a high portion of their output over the years and invested it in physical capital and education. Throughout the 1960s and 1970s, Japan was investing more than 30 percent of gross output, while the United States was investing less than 20 percent. In 1985, Japan invested 28 percent in gross capital formation and the United States invested 19 percent of gross domestic product (GDP) (see table 10.1). Such differences indicate that Japanese growth is indeed likely to continue at a faster pace than in the United States.

Confirmation of higher income in Japan as a result of cumulative investment and continued investment activity comes from a variety of

Table 10.1
Comparative Data for Japan and the United States

Subject of Comparison		Japan	United States
Gross National Product at the end of 1989 (billions of dollars, using exchange rate)		$ 2,807	$ 5,340
College Enrollment per 100	Males 20-24	38.2	57.3[a]
	Females 20-24	20.7	
Life Expectancy	Male	74.54	71.00
	Female	80.18	78.30
1985 Housing Land Prices Relative to 1960 Prices		15.3	4.4
Scientists & Engineers in Research & Development		531,612	728,600
Stock Market Capitalization at Year End 1989 (billions of dollars)		$ 3,850	$ 3,010
Exports in 1987			
By country, giving the top four export markets of Japan and the United States (millions of dollars)			
	Japan	NA	$27,797
	United States	$84,232	NA
	South Korea	$13,214	$ 7,660
	West Germany	$12,832	$11,514
	China	$ 8,249	$ 3,488
	Canada	$ 5,611	$59,212
	Mexico	$ 1,389	$14,573
	United Kingdom	$ 8,400	$13,797
By commodity, giving the top four export categories of Japan and the United States (millions of dollars)			
	Office Machines	$18,053	$19,969
	Telecommunications, Sound Equipment	$25,156	$ 5,637
	Electric Machinery, NES	$22,030	$17,854
	Road Vehicles	$58,822	$22,038
	Other Transport Equipment	$ 5,109	$19,201

Table 10.1 (continued)

Subject of Comparison		Japan	United States
Imports in 1987			
By country giving the top four exporting countries to Japan and the United States (millions of dollars)			
	Japan		$88,072
	United States	$31,691	
	Saudi Arabia	$ 7,311	$ 4,903
	Indonesia	$ 8,427	$ 3,719
	West Germany	$ 6,116	$28,020
	Canada	$ 5,761	$70,644
	Mexico	$ 1,625	$20,511
By commodity, giving the top four import categories of Japan and the United States (millions of dollars)			
	Fish	$ 7,992	$ 5,872
	Cork & Wood	$ 7,065	$ 3,528
	Metalliferous Ores, Scrap	$ 6,132	$ 2,597
	Petroleum & Products	$27,897	$43,984
	Electric Machinery, NES	$ 3,715	$25,365
	Road Vehicles	$ 2,582	$74,580
	Clothing & Accessories	$ 4,674	$22,116
Trade Barriers in 1987 (ad valorem percentage)			
	Tariffs	6.2	3.3
	Non-Tariff Barriers	8.2	2.4
Economic Performance in the 1980s (percentage)			
	Average Unemployment	2.5	7.6
	Average Inflation	2.7	5.8
	Average Real Growth (total)	3.8	2.6
	Average Real Growth (per capita)	3.2	1.6
Other Economic Variables as of 1985			
	Operating Surplus as percentage of GDP	24	19
	Gross Capital Formation (as percentage of GDP)	28	19

Sources: Honeygold (1989); OECD (1989); Office of the Prime Minister, *Japan Statistical Yearbook,* various years; Saxonhouse and Stern (1989); U.N. *Yearbook of International Trade Statistics,* and *Yearbook of National Account Statistics,* various years; United States, *Economic Report of the President,* various years.

[a] The United States enrollment rate is for men and women.

indicators. Presently, Japan's life expectancy is higher than in the United States for both men and women. Data from 1983 and 1984 indicate a Japanese man can expect to live an extra 3.5 years. Japanese women can expect to live an extra 1.9 years (see table 10.1).

Japan has a higher proportion of its work force working as scientists and engineers in research and experimental development. Japan had 531,612 workers in this category in 1984, while the United States had 728,600 (United Nations *Statistical Yearbook,* 1985/86). Japan's total work force was 60 million in 1985 and the United States' was 117 million (see table 1.1). This gives Japan 8.9 scientific and engineering researchers per 1,000 workers. The United States had 6.2 scientific and engineering researchers per 1,000 workers. Consequently, we might expect Japanese companies to be cost effective in engineering and designing their products. Nevertheless, the United States will probably continue to make more overall innovations with its larger number of researchers. The comparisons made here show how two friendly rivals are likely to do relative to each other. However, while innovative technology lends temporary advantage to a company or country, it is important to remember that all of humankind ultimately can benefit from such advances. Technology is transferred around the world and enhances efficiency.

Japan is still a net importer of technology. Japan had receipts of $746 million in 1985 and payments of $2,522 million for international transactions in technology (*Japan Statistical Yearbook,* 1987). Receipts for technology transactions were only 30 percent of payments. This was up from 23 percent in 1975, but shows that Japan as still paying more for technology than it is paid. Japan will probably have this ratio continue to rise.

Japan has a strong educational system in place that will further its economic growth and development. It is not clear whether it will make more of a contribution to growth than the U.S. system does. Virtually all children in the United States and Japan get some secondary education. Japanese secondary school students do much better on international math and science exams than American students. Top Japanese students scored 65 percent on science exams, while top students in the United States only scored 52 percent on these exams. Japanese students had the advantage of having been taught 92 percent of the items tested for, as opposed to only 55 percent for the U.S. students (National Center for Education Statistics, 1989).

The United States' strength in education comes at the college level. Far more young people go on to college in the United States than in Japan. Of those aged 20–24 in the United States, 57 percent have enrolled in college. For this age group in Japan, 38 percent of males and only 21 percent of females have enrolled in college (*Japan Statistical Yearbook,* 1987). Monk-Turner and Baba (1987) indicate that Japan still underutilizes the talents of women. Most of the women attending college in Japan are in two-year special schools.

When income is measured by the amount of goods and services that can be purchased in the local economy, Japanese income is not as high as when simply translated by exchange rates. According to Balassa and Noland (1988), Japan's purchasing power parity per capita GDP in 1987 was 81 percent of the level in the United States. I adjusted these figures for changes in real income per worker in the United States and Japan since 1987 as reported in the *OECD Economic Outlook.* In 1990, the real purchasing power per capita income in Japan was 85 percent of real per capita income in the United States. In conclusion, Japanese per capita income is somewhere between 85 and 110 percent of the level in the United States in real terms, depending on how you measure it.

WEALTH

Wealth consists of ownership claims to factors of production or financial instruments. Society's wealth consists of the factors of production, because the purely financial instruments net out. A bond, for instance, stipulates that agent A owes agent B certain payments in consequence of agent B extending certain payments to A at an earlier time. Measured wealth is the present value of the future income streams that are expected to accrue to the various assets. Present value is usually determined in an active secondary market for stocks and bonds. Real estate is more often valued by appraisals based on sales of comparable properties, since no two properties are identical in the same way that two stock certificates are identical.

Wealth tends to fluctuate more in value than income does because of the complications in its determination:

1. Expected income streams are more volatile than actual income streams as people go through periods of optimism and pessimism.
2. Present value calculations change when the pure rate of time discount changes. A dollar today is generally worth more than a dollar next year, but not always to the same degree.
3. The confidence investors have in their own expectations can vary and this affects present value calculations of expected income streams.

(See Poterba and Summers, 1988; Shiller, 1984; and Turner, 1990.)

Wealth of one country also fluctuates with respect to other countries with changes in exchange rates. Since portfolio holdings of assets can change very fast, relative wealth among countries is an even more precarious concept to measure than relative income. If investors in Japan seek to acquire assets in the United States, they sell assets in Japan, convert yen to dollars, and buy assets in the United States. As long as only a few investors choose to undertake such transactions, market prices do not change a great deal and the switch in assets occurs for the individual as desired.

When many Japanese investors want to undertake such transactions at the same time, complications arise. A large number of Japanese investors trying to sell Japanese assets at the same time will drive down the price of those assets. As asset prices fall in Japan, for a given expected future income from an asset, the higher the expected return on the asset. As a large amount of yen is converted to dollars, this will tend to cause the yen/dollar exchange rate to rise. Essentially, the dollar's value rises because more people want dollars to undertake their desired transactions. As a large number of Japanese investors buy assets in the United States, those asset prices rise. This means that, with given expected income streams from U.S. assets, the expected return on those assets will fall. The overall effects of such a surge in Japanese preference for U.S. assets is threefold: (1) Japanese assets measured in yen decline, (2) U.S. assets measured in dollars increase, and (3) the international purchasing power of a dollar is strengthened vis-à-vis the yen.

It is easy to see why speculative surges across borders can be so disruptive. If an investor can anticipate such a surge, then by acting before others, she can avoid a loss in yen, earn a gain in dollars, and benefit from the rise in the dollar versus the yen. On the other hand, if the surge is temporary and all values return to their original position, someone who changed investments during the middle of the surge would have received a lower price for yen assets, paid too much for U.S. assets, and suffered a fall in the relative value of dollar holdings. Policymakers as well as investors are concerned with potential disturbances to markets from changes in international portfolios.

Japanese stock market valuation was 28 percent greater than the market value of U.S. stocks at the end of 1989. Using 1987 year-end estimates reported by Honeygold (1989) and updated using data from the International Monetary Fund's *International Financial Statistics,* Japanese equity markets were estimated to be $3,850 billion at the end of 1989. U.S. equity markets were estimated to be $3,010 billion.

The relative value of the two markets has switched in 1990. The United States has regained its position as having the largest equity market. By September 18, 1990, the Tokyo stock market (Nikkei) had lost 38.62 percent of its value since December 31, 1989. The U.S. market (Standard & Poor's 500) had lost 9.85 percent since year-end 1989. The yen/dollar exchange rate on September 18, 1990 was 137.85 (*The Wall Street Journal,*

September 19, 1990). The year-end yen/dollar rate was 143.45 (International Financial Statistics). This gives Japan's market value of stocks as of September 18, 1990 as:

$$\$3{,}850 \text{ billion} \times 143 \text{ yen/\$} \times (1 - .3862)/138 \text{ yen/\$} = \$2{,}449 \text{ billion}$$

The U.S. market value of stocks at September 18, 1990 is:

$$\$3{,}010 \text{ billion} \times (1 - .0985) = \$2{,}714 \text{ billion}$$

The U.S. market is now 10 percent greater than the Japanese market. The two markets could well seesaw back and forth for the claim to be the number one global equity market.

Unless there is a collapse in Japanese land values, there will be no such dispute about the number one real estate market. The value of Japanese land is four times the value of all the land in the United States (Hayashi, 1989; Moffatt, 1990). This is in spite of the fact that the United States has more than twenty-five times as much land as Japan. Part of the reason is the protectionist agriculture of Japan as discussed in chapter 5. As shown in table 10.1, Japanese housing land prices went up to more than fifteen times their 1960 prices. Shelter prices in the United States went up to 4.4 times their 1960 level over this same period.

Real estate is the ultimate nontraded good. Even though the ownership claims can change hands, the land itself stays where it is (erosion aside). Relative valuation of real estate is therefore especially prone to domestic market distortions. Changes in policies or preferences could cause major shifts in valuation. The value placed on land by the Japanese is what will continue to set its price.

COMPARATIVE TRADE PATTERNS

The United States and Japan are important to each other as trading partners. They are also intense export competitors. The most important trading partners of Japan are not the most important to the United States in terms of either exports or imports. The most important export commodities for Japan also tend to be the most important to the United States. The most important import commodities for Japan tend not to be the most important for the United States.

Exports

The United States is Japan's largest export market. In 1987, Japan exported $84.2 billion to the United States, which represented 37 percent of Japan's exports (for this and related data, see table 10.1). The United

States exported $27.8 billion to Japan in 1987, which was 11 percent of U.S. exports. This makes Japan the second-largest export market for the United States.

After the United States, the next-largest export markets for Japan are South Korea, West Germany, and China. South Korea received 6 percent of Japan's exports, West Germany received 6 percent, and China received 4 percent. None of these three countries is among the top four export markets of the United States.

The top four export markets for the United States are Canada, Japan, Mexico, and the United Kingdom. Canada received 23 percent of U.S. exports; Japan received 11 percent; Mexico received 6 percent; and the United Kingdom got 5 percent. West Germany is the only country in Japan's top four list that almost received enough exports from the United States to be among its top four export markets.

Nothing is magical about the number 4, but by looking at a few markets that are very important to each country, we can see that Japan and the United States have very different trade patterns. A lot of the difference appears to be explained by proximity. Canada and Mexico are adjacent to the United States. They receive about 29 percent of U.S. exports and only 3 percent of Japan's exports. South Korea and China are a short sea voyage from Japan. They receive about 10 percent of Japan's exports and only 4 percent of U.S. exports.

There is a great deal more overlap in the major commodities exported by Japan and the United States than there is in the major countries to which they export. Of the top four commodity categories exported by Japan in 1987, three of them are also among the top four commodity categories exported by the United States. The two-digit Standard International Trade Categories (SITC) that had the most Japanese exports were 75—office machines, 76—telecommunications and sound equipment, 77—electric machinery, and 78—road vehicles. All of these except 76—telecommunications and sound equipment were among the top four commodity categories exported by the United States. The additional top export category for the United States was 79—other transport equipment. U.S. exports of airplanes account for the largest part of its SITC 79 exports.

Road vehicles are the largest export category for both Japan and the United States. Japan exported $58.8 billion of road vehicles, which was 26 percent of Japan's exports. The United States exported $22.0 billion of road vehicles, which was 9 percent of its exports. It is clear that Japan's exports are greater in this category, but U.S. road vehicle exports are clearly important.

Japan has overwhelming superiority over the United States in the net exports of road vehicles. Japan exported $58.8 billion and imported $2.6 billion, for net exports of $56.2 billion of road vehicles. The United States exported $22.0 billion and imported $74.6 billion, for net exports of $-52.6 billion. As is well known to American consumers, Japan is very competitive in the global automobile market.

The second-largest export category for Japan is telecommunications and sound equipment, with 11 percent of Japanese exports. U.S. exports in this category are only 2 percent of its total exports. VCRs, televisions, and audio equipment are consumer areas in which Japan has dominated the global market.

The third-largest export category for Japan is electric machinery, with 10 percent of exports. This is the fourth-largest export category for the United States, with 7 percent of total exports. Electric machinery is also the third-largest import category for the United States, with 6 percent of U.S. imports in this category. Again, in an area of competition with the Japanese, Japan wins in terms of total exports and net exports. Japan exported $22.0 billion and the United States exported $17.9 billion. Japan imported $3.7 billion of electric machinery and the United States imported $25.4 billion. This gives Japan net exports of $18.3 billion and the United States net imports of $7.6 billion of electric machinery.

Japan's fourth-largest export category in 1987 was office machines, with 8 percent of exports. Office machines also had 8 percent of U.S. exports, with $20.0 billion, which made it the second-largest United States export category. U.S. exports in office machines were $1.8 billion more than Japan's in 1987. Neither country had office machines as one of their top four import groups.

Other transport equipment only accounted for 2 percent of Japan's exports. It was the third-largest export category for the United States, with 8 percent of exports. U.S. exports of planes and other transport equipment exceeded Japan's by $14.1 billion in 1987.

Imports

West Germany is the only country among the top four providers of imports to both the United States and Japan. The top four exporters to Japan are the United States (22% of Japan's imports), Indonesia (6%), Saudi Arabia (5%), and West Germany (4%). The top four exporters to the United States are Japan (21% of U.S. imports), Canada (17%), West Germany (7%), and Mexico (5%).

Petroleum and related products is the only two-digit SITC commodity category in the four categories of imports for both Japan and the United States. The United States and Japan vie with each other for export markets to a much greater extent than they vie for imports. Petroleum and related products was 19 percent of Japan's imports and 10 percent of U.S. imports in 1987. The other top imports for Japan were fish (5%), cork and wood (5%), and ores and scrap (4%). Each of these categories accounted for less than 1 percent of U.S. imports. The other top import categories for the United States were road vehicles (18%), electric machinery (6%), and clothing (5%). Each of these categories accounted for 2–3 percent of Japan's imports.

Trade Barriers

Japanese trade barriers have declined in most areas over the last two decades. In chapter 5, we explored these barriers at some length. Saxonhouse and Stern (1989) report an average tariff of 6.2 percent for Japan and 3.3 percent for the United States. They also report 8.2 percent as an average tariff equivalent of nontariff barriers in Japan and 2.4 percent average tariff equivalent in the United States.

The Japanese barriers are primarily in the agriculture and food area. The U.S. barriers are mostly in textiles, steel, and transport equipment. Using customs duties divided by total imports instead of the weights used by Saxonhouse and Stern results in an average ratio of 2.6 percent for Japan and 3.3 percent for the United States in 1986 (Japan Institute for Social and Economic Affairs, 1988, p. 31). The existing barriers are important for selected industries (especially rice farming), but are relatively low by historical standards.

OVERALL ECONOMIC FUNCTIONING

Japan has done much better than the United States at achieving macroeconomic goals. Virtually all economic policymakers in market economies (and centrally planned ones also, for that matter) want to achieve low unemployment, low inflation, and high economic growth rates. In the 1980s, Japan has performed better by all these measures than has the United States (see table 10.1 for the following data).

Japan's average unemployment rate in the 1980s was 2.5 percent. The U.S. rate was 7.6 percent on average. The U.S. rate is more than three times the Japanese rate. Since unemployment is a measure of lost production, it is clearly important to keep unemployment low to achieve productive efficiency.

Some policymakers would choose a somewhat higher unemployment rate, in order to curb inflation. Japan, however, achieved a lower inflation rate than the United States in spite of lower unemployment. Japan's average inflation rate in the 1980s was 2.7 percent, compared to the U.S. rate of 5.8 percent. The U.S. rate is 2.1 times the Japanese rate. At the U.S. rate, prices would double every 12.5 years; it would take twenty-six years for prices to double at the Japanese inflation rate in the 1980s.

Average real per capita growth in Japan was approximately double the rate in the United States. Japan's average real growth rate for the 1980s was 3.8 percent, compared to the U.S. rate of 2.6 percent. Population growth in Japan was slightly lower than in the United States, however. Consequently, the per capita real growth rate in Japan was 3.2 percent, while the United States had a real per capita growth rate of 1.6 percent. At the Japanese rate, real per capita income will double in about twenty-two years, while at the U.S. rate, it will take approximately forty-five years for real per capita income to double.

A primary reason for Japan's faster real income growth is its greater rate of investment in productive capacity. In 1985, Japan invested 28 percent of its GDP in gross capital formation. Gross capital formation does not net out depreciation of existing plant, and is higher than net capital formation. The United States invested only 19 percent of GDP in gross capital formation. Japan's operating surplus was 24 percent of GDP in 1985, while the level in the United States was 19 percent. Operating surplus is approximately net profits plus interest and rents. Higher operating surpluses indicate higher returns to physical capital all else equal.

SUMMARY

The United States has had a relative decline in its income in the global economy over the last forty years. Japan has had a dramatic increase in its relative income, largely due to its high investment rate. As Japan's per capita income has approached or exceeded (depending on how it is measured) per capita income in the United States, there have been increased feelings of hostility against Japan.

Japan's economic growth is the result of sustained investment in plant, equipment, and education. Japan will increasingly contribute to the technological progress in the global economy. Even if Japan's per capita income exceeds that of the United States in real terms, the United States will continue to benefit from its relationship with Japan.

Japan has the highest wealth in the world measured at market prices. The Japanese real estate market is greater than that in the United States in total value. The Japanese stock market is sometimes valued higher than the U.S. stock market. The income stream of Japanese assets is less than the income stream from such assets in the United States. The higher valuation of Japanese assets comes from the lower discount rate applied to the expected future income from these assets.

The United States is the largest exporter to Japan and it is also Japan's largest export market. Japan and the United States compete in export markets. Their major export categories overlap. At the present time, Japan seems to have been able to gain exports at the expense of the U.S. share. The falling value of the dollar will tend to make U.S. goods more competitive. However, by the same token, a falling dollar tends to lower

U.S. relative income and wealth. Japanese and U.S. trade barriers still exist, but they have tended to decrease over most of the postwar period.

Japanese macroeconomic performance in the 1980s has been superior to that in the United States. Japanese unemployment has been lower, with lower inflation. Economic growth has been faster than in the United States. Japanese investment for future output continues to exceed that of the United States.

11 Japan and Less Developed Countries

Japan has a major interest in the orderly development of the world's less developed countries (LDCs). Changes in multilateral institutions that further dynamic efficiency will benefit LDCs the most, but such changes can also benefit countries like Japan that are net lenders. Trade between Japan and LDCs has the archetypical pattern of comparative advantage, and is mutually beneficial as a consequence. Japan also provides a potent role model for developing countries.

Japanese relationships with LDCs are complex. Japanese exports to and imports from selected LDCs and regions are described below. Japanese foreign direct investment in LDCs has been of major importance to some LDCs. Japan has increased its official development assistance, and is now roughly on a par with the United States in terms of the total amount of aid.

DYNAMIC GLOBAL EFFICIENCY

Dynamic global efficiency requires that the allocation of resources to individuals over time and space achieve the condition of "Pareto efficiency." Pareto efficiency requires that no one can be made better off without others being made worse off. Even in an efficient world, society might want to reallocate resources to achieve a more just or equitable result (Rawls, 1971; Buchanan and Tullock, 1967). Income transfers to the sick and infirm might be made on a voluntary basis if equity is the only issue. However, if the global economy is not dynamically efficient, stronger mechanisms for moving the system toward efficiency might benefit all participants.

LDCs have a lower average level of education, less physical capital per worker, and a lower level of technological efficiency than countries with higher income per capita. Improvements in all three of these areas require substantial investment. Investment in education or human capital is probably the most essential, and also the most costly. Besides the funds for providing teachers and educational facilities, it is necessary for some or all of the time of the young to be free to pursue an education. In a life where people are barely surviving, every worker is pressed into service no matter how meager the rewards. The longer-run benefits of an education may not be enough of an inducement to send the young to school if insufficient financial resources are available to families in LDCs.

Equipment, machinery, and other capital goods are required for a high level of output per worker. The technology and the specific technological know-how of production processes have to be available. Licensing technology and acquiring the necessary equipment can require a lot of financial resources. In a country with low income, even a high savings rate would generate a fairly small amount of financial resources per person. It is the investment of savings in human and physical capital that permits higher levels of production in the future.

Many LDCs do not have well-developed capital markets. Capital markets serve the purpose of transferring financial resources from savers to investors. The presence of secondary markets for stocks and bonds encourages the overall issuance of such stocks and bonds. If the buyer of a bond or stock knows that he cannot sell it without extended private negotiations, he will not pay as much for it. This is the same as saying that he will require a higher expected return before he will buy such a security. Consequently, many firms in LDCs will have a higher cost of capital than comparable firms in high-income countries. In some cases, outside capital will simply not be available to firms at any price.

The capital problems of large and medium-sized firms in LDCs are small compared to the capital problems of poorly educated individuals. In most high-income countries, schooling is required at the elementary level for all children. This universal schooling is paid for by the state and is supported by taxes. In many LDCs, such schooling is not universally provided. It is beyond the resources of the individual family to arrange for such schooling. Teachers, with an advanced education, would earn a relatively high income in many LDCs compared with their relative position in high-income countries. This is because of the relative scarcity of their skills.

Education in LDCs requires a greatly increased flow of resources to even approach that available in the high-income countries. It is virtually impossible for this educational opportunity to be privately financed. The periods of investment before a positive payback would be too long. The contract providing for repayment of the educational loan could not presently guarantee performance. Further, if the educational facilities were to be provided as a result of increased private demand coming from private financing, the debt of the whole country would be increasing too fast (Turner, 1987). Lenders would fear country-wide default even if individuals were willing to pay. LDCs might also hesitate to guarantee financing, because individuals frequently leave LDCs after attaining an education (Bhagwati, 1976).

In a global, dynamically efficient economy, the cost of borrowing would approximate the rate paid to lenders regardless of country of residence. If some countries had greater variability of income that increased risk, then such risk could be insured against. The result would be a world in which available resources are allocated to those uses with the highest rates of return. The risk of default needs to be minimized in order to attain efficiency in a dynamic system. The difference between borrowing and lending rates should be limited to transaction costs, fair insurance against hazards (like the death of the borrower), and a minimal arbitrage profit for sharing the risk of making resources available from one point in time and space to another point in time and space. Such an efficient system would lower the rates paid by marginal borrowers and raise rates paid to lenders.

Dynamic efficiency also requires free trade. Besides the resource flows that would occur with improvement of the international capital market, LDCs would need assurance of access to all the world's markets. Investment in plant and equipment and even human capital takes many years to pay off. Since LDCs tend to have low per capita income, their own domestic markets may not be very extensive for many goods. This makes LDCs especially dependent on global markets. If changes in the global economy can easily shut off markets for LDC goods, then there are few incentives to invest in LDC plants. A stable, dependable market is essential for goods that can be produced by LDCs. Free trade, perfected capital markets, and a free flow of technology would greatly accelerate economic growth in LDCs.

Technology transfers to LDCs are essential for rapid growth. Such transfers can take place through licensing, direct investment, educational activities, and other means. Sometimes the technology can be transferred intact, but substantial modifications may be necessary. The relative factor returns are generally quite different in LDCs. The relative wage for semiskilled labor is usually much lower in LDCs than it is in the advanced industrial countries. Production processes that are most economically efficient in LDCs would use relatively more semiskilled labor than production processes in advanced industrial countries. Unfortunately, the LDCs do not always possess the necessary engineering and entrepreneurial talent to make the needed adjustments.

Dynamic global efficiency can be increased by factor mobility. Machinery and equipment can move from Japan to China, for instance, or Chinese people could move to Japan to have access to plant and equipment. The purposes of both these kinds of factor movements can, at least theoretically, be achieved by free trade between China and Japan. Presently, restrictions on labor migrations are severe. However, with freer trade and enhanced capital flows, large labor migration should not be necessary to give LDC residents greater opportunity for higher real incomes.

THE STRUCTURE OF JAPAN'S RELATIONSHIP WITH LDCs

Japan tends to run a substantial trade deficit with LDCs. Japan also provides substantial foreign direct investment to LDCs. Japan is one of the largest foreign aid donors among the advanced industrial economies. All of these attributes mean that Japan is furthering the development of LDCs.

Japan provides LDCs a market for many of their goods. The excess foreign exchange they earn with Japan can then be used to buy other needed commodities from the United States, the European Community, and other nations and regions of the world. Japanese investment and development assistance also lets LDCs undertake investment more rapidly than would otherwise be possible.

Japan's Trading and Investment Relations with LDCs

In 1985, Japan's imports of food, crude materials, fuel, and basic manufactured goods were 76 percent of its total imports. These are generally goods where LDCs have a comparative advantage. Fuels are a special case, since when prices are high, some OPEC countries have high incomes and are not like LDCs. The Japanese market looms large for LDCs.

Japan received 6 percent of the world's imports in 1985, but its share of imports that originated in LDCs was much higher. Japan received 47 percent of the exports from Indonesia, 24 percent of Saudi Arabia's exports, and 35 percent of exports from the United Arab Emirates in 1985. Approximately 21 percent of China's exports went to Japan in 1985.

Japan as a market is especially crucial for Indonesia. As shown in table 11.1, in 1987, Japanese imports from Indonesia were $8.4 billion. Japanese exports were $3.0 billion to Indonesia. This left Indonesia with a trade surplus with Japan of $5.4 billion. In addition, Japan had $.5 billion of foreign direct investment in Indonesia in 1987, and provided $.6 billion in aid. The result was that Indonesia had the capability to buy up to

Table 11.1
Japan and Developing Countries: Investment, Assistance, and Trade

	1987 Japanese Exports	1987 Japanese Imports	1987 Japanese Foreign Direct Investment	1987 Japanese Official Development Assistance
China	$ 8,249	$ 7,386	$ 1,226	$ 527
Hong Kong	$ 8,865	$ 1,557	$ 1,072	NA
India	$ 1,957	$ 1,530	NA	$ 349
Indonesia	$ 2,990	$ 8,427	$ 545	$ 639
South Korea	$ 13,214	$ 8,058	$ 647	$ 171
Pakistan	$ 936	$ 492	NA	$ 163
Singapore	$ 5,947	$ 2,023	$ 494	NA
Other Asia	$ 27,989	$ 36,931	$ 884	NA
Brazil	$ 878	$ 2,032	$ 229	$ 67
Mexico	$ 1,389	$ 1,625	$ 28	$ 59
Other Latin America	$ 5,790	$ 2,493	$ 4,559	NA
Egypt	$ 544	$ 220	NA	$ 134
Other Africa	$ 4,692	$ 3,453	$ 272	NA
Total for Listed Countries and Regions	$ 83,440	$ 76,227	$ 9,956	$2,109
World Total	$229,054	$146,048	$33,364	$7,425

Sources: Japan Economic Institute, JEI Report no. 31A, August 11, 1989, and JEI Report no. 41A, October 27, 1989; and United Nations, *Yearbook of International Trade Statistics, 1987.*

Note: Dollar figures are in millions of U.S. dollars.

$6.5 billion of goods and services from the rest of the world because of its relationship with Japan. This is in addition to Indonesia's export earnings or capital inflow from the rest of the world.

Chinese trade with Japan was in deficit in 1987. Japan exported $8.2 billion to China and imported $7.4 billion. The $.8 billion deficit was less than the $1.2 billion of Japanese direct investment and $.5 billion of official aid. As a result, China could buy $.9 billion of goods from the rest of the world because of Japan.

Hong Kong, Korea, and Singapore all had substantial deficits with Japan. Undoubtedly, part of the reason is that Japan ships parts and machinery to these countries for production of goods that go to other export markets. Japan exported $28.0 billion to these three countries and imported $11.6 billion, for a Japanese surplus of $16.4 billion. These countries received $2.2 billion of foreign direct investment. These countries thus act as a conduit for purchasing power of $14.2 billion to flow to Japan.

Pakistan and India had trade deficits with Japan in 1987. Their imports from Japan were $2.9 billion and their exports to Japan were $2.0 billion. They received official aid from Japan of $.5 billion, which was not as much as the $.9 billion trade deficit. Consequently, they relied on other global sources of liquid funding for their purchasing power.

Other Asian countries such as Malaysia and Thailand ran a trade surplus with Japan in 1987. Japan exported $28.0 billion to other Asian countries and imported $36.9 billion. Japan also had $.9 billion of foreign direct investment in other Asian countries. Consequently, these countries could use $9.8 billion of purchasing power in the rest of the world because of their relationship with Japan.

Japan ran trade deficits with Brazil and Mexico in 1987. Japan exported $2.3 billion to these two countries and imported $3.7 billion from them. Japan also had foreign direct investment of $.3 billion and development assistance of $.1 billion in these countries. Brazil and Mexico increased their purchasing power from the rest of the world by $1.8 billion due to their relationship with Japan.

Other Latin American countries, primarily offshore banking centers, ran substantial balance of trade deficits with Japan in 1987. Japan exported $5.8 billion to these countries and imported $2.5 from them. However, Japan's foreign direct investment in these countries of $4.6 billion resulted in their having $1.3 billion overall to spend in the rest of the world because of their relationship with Japan.

Egypt and other African countries ran trade deficits with Japan in 1987. Japan exported $5.2 billion to Africa and imported $3.7 billion. Japanese foreign direct investment and official aid was not sufficient to cover the $1.5 billion trade deficit. Africa did not gain global purchasing power because of its relationship with Japan.

In 1987, Japan ran a trade surplus on average with the countries and regions listed in table 11.1. Japanese total exports to these areas were $83.4 billion, while Japanese imports from these areas were $76.2 billion. This $7.2 billion Japanese trade surplus is less than the $10.0 billion in foreign direct investment by Japan in these areas. More than $2 billion of Japanese aid was also given to these areas. In total, the listed areas had more purchasing power for use in the rest of the world because of their relationship with Japan.

The trade deficits of the listed areas with Japan were relatively smaller than the rest of the world's deficits with Japan. Exports from these areas to Japan were 91 percent of their imports from Japan in 1987. Japan's imports from the world as a whole were only 64 percent of Japan's exports in 1987. When Japan's overall trade is balanced (no surplus or deficit), the LDCs will be running surpluses with Japan.

Japan's Special Role for Development of LDCs

Japan can provide the most assistance to LDCs by maintaining and furthering an open and dependable trading system. The nature of development is to go through periods of rapid adjustment. Comparative advantage will shift as various factors of production change. Capital equipment, human skills, and education take long periods of time to pay off. Such investments will more readily be made if LDCs are assured of open access to all the major markets in the global economy. LDCs need to develop along dynamically efficient paths that maximize their potential. This requires assurance that success in their own export industries will not bring about restrictions against such exports.

The Japanese are well aware of the potential pitfalls of success at pursuing a global export strategy of development. Japan's rapid growth in the postwar period has resulted in many countries discriminating against Japanese goods. Japan's success has lowered the relative prices of those goods where it has a comparative advantage. Industries affected in other countries have bitterly fought Japanese access to their domestic markets. The greatest service the Japanese can do for LDCs is to reduce the extent to which such actions occur against quickly growing LDC industries, whether textiles or electronic components. This requires action to keep Japanese markets open and also to keep the global trading system as open as possible.

Japanese imports from Africa, Asia, and Latin America are more than $75 billion and growing. Exporting from these countries to Japan is an essential way for these countries to earn the resources to pay for various physical and social investments. Even when growth of exports from LDCs to Japan causes disruption in Japan's domestic markets, the policy of openness to trade needs to be honored.

As LDCs develop, Japan is likely to benefit a great deal. The exchanges of goods between Japan and LDCs occur largely along the lines of comparative advantage. The growing income in LDCs will provide greater markets for Japanese exports, and growing imports from LDCs will increase the real income of Japanese consumers. If Japan and other countries are able to strengthen the global trading system, Japan's trade with other developed economies will also benefit.

Japan is now the world's largest creditor nation and is likely to remain so for the indefinite future. The allocation of Japan's investment resources is critically important to the LDCs. From a global economic efficiency point of view, net capital flows from Japan to LDCs should help these countries in the development process. We saw in chapter 8, though, that most capital was flowing from Japan to the United States and other high income countries. The United States hopefully will reverse its net capital draw from global capital markets. It is well enough developed to provide developmental resources to the rest of the world rather than require such resources. If the United States does reduce its use of global financial capital, there will be more capital available, from Japan and other countries, and at a lower rate of interest for investment in LDCs.

Japan is a high saving country and as such can benefit from a dynamic growth in LDCs. If Japan provides additional resources to LDCs now, it will be able to enjoy higher living standards in the future. Long-term investment in LDCs should pay rich financial rewards. A key element in such a positive outcome is improvement in institutional arrangements to ensure completion of contracts. Japanese investors will not want to see investments lost to default any more than other investors. It is essential that multilateral mechanisms be functioning to smooth cross-border investments. It is most important for the benefit to LDCs, but it is also crucial to Japan's long-run benefit.

Japan's role goes beyond that of providing capital for development. Japan is also a technological leader in many industries. The transfer of this technology to LDCs can bring enormous benefits to these countries. Whether such transfer takes place through licensing, foreign direct investment, or some other mechanism is secondary to the importance that it take place. Projecting ahead, it is reasonable to conclude that Japan's rate of technical progress will continue at a fast clip. LDCs will benefit if they share in such technological gains.

Japan's success in its own development is sure to encourage LDCs to try similar paths. A trading economy that exports to a global market has succeeded for Japan. It is likely that similar market-oriented export strategies will also benefit other countries seeking rapid development. Mexico seems to be trying to adopt such a strategy now. Changes in Eastern Europe, China, and other countries in Latin America also seem to be moving in the direction of producing for the global economy. Japan's success is certainly one of the motivations for such changes. Japan's increased development assistance and investment, together with an openness to LDC exports, can help assure the success of the development of those countries that take this approach.

SUMMARY

Japan has shown what a country can achieve by investing substantial resources in its own development in an open trading environment. Japan has produced for export markets as well as its own domestic market. It has provided an alternative model to development through import substitution. It has been tremendously successful, and thereby provides encouragement to LDCs to take a development path of production for the global market.

Dynamic efficiency in the global economy is far from being realized. It will be fostered, however, if capital flows to a greater degree from Japan and other net lender countries to LDCs. For LDCs to be able to borrow and invest, they need to have reasonable assurance of open global markets in the future. Japan and the LDCs have a natural alliance in promoting a free trade regime. Japan's imports are heavily weighted toward the goods in which LDCs have a comparative advantage.

In a more balanced trading environment, Japan would run a trade deficit with LDCs. It would run a trade surplus with the United States and other developed economies. Comparative advantage will change for various countries that are now LDCs, just as it has for Japan. As these changes occur, they can be furthered by the transfer of technology from Japan, the United States, the EEC, and other countries. All countries can benefit from the further development of human skills and talents in all the countries of the world.

12 Japan's Place in the Dynamic Global Economy

Japan has been the fastest growing of the major global economies over the post-World War II period. Japan's share of the gross national product (GNP) of the world's market economies has gone from 3 percent in 1955 to 12 percent in 1985. At the present investment rates in various countries, Japan's share of global GNP will continue to get larger. Japan's growth has largely come about from a very high rate of investment. Japan has invested in plant and equipment at rates substantially higher than the United States and other advanced economies. Japan has also invested large sums in human capital.

Japan's tremendous increase in per capita income is almost a case study in the power of compound interest. The returns the Japanese received for their investment were in terms of higher output per worker. Since Japanese savings rates remained high over the last forty years, the Japanese investment in Japan's own productive capacity continued to increase at a compound rate. The result is a Japan with per capita income close to or greater than that of the United States today, compared with per capita income of about 10 percent of the U.S. level in 1955.

Japan's rapid growth has had large repercussions on its trading partners. Japan's pattern of comparative advantage has changed in major ways over the last forty years because of its rapid rate of investment. Trade barriers in Japan and other countries have been generally lowered over this time period. Serious impediments to trade still exist, however, both on Japan's exports and its imports.

Japan has been relatively successful at maintaining a macroeconomic balance in its high-growth economy. High real growth frequently causes high inflation and trade deficits. Japan has avoided these twin plagues and has maintained high employment as well.

Japan's higher growth, savings, and income have resulted in Japan becoming a dominant financial power in the global economy. Japan's financial markets are now a major source of financial capital. Investment in Japanese markets by foreigners is also of major importance today. Forty years ago, Japanese financial markets had little effect on the global economy.

Japan has had a special relationship with the United States. It continues to have strong defense, trade, and financial ties to the United States. Japan's relationships with less developed countries (LDCs) are important as trading partner, financier, provider of aid, and as a "model for development." As Japan's growth has continued, it has become increasingly important in all these areas.

JAPAN AND GLOBAL TRADE

Japan's rapid growth in the postwar period has had a profound impact on its trading partners. Japan's exports are increasing their penetration of global markets. Japan's economy is critically dependent on imports of food, material, and fuel. Japanese imports are becoming increasingly important to those countries exporting to Japan. Japan and its trading partners have lowered their trade barriers over the postwar period, but many such barriers still distort trade.

Japanese Exports

Japan's share of world exports was only 2 percent in 1955, and is 10 percent today. Japan now provides more than 20 percent of U.S. imports, compared to only 4 percent in 1955. Countries on the Pacific Rim now get 25 percent or more of their imports from Japan, compared to much smaller shares in 1955. The members of the European Economic Community (EEC) still only acquire about 5 percent of their imports from Japan, but even that is up sharply from what was provided by Japan in 1955.

The increased share of Japanese goods in various markets has led to many complaints about unfair Japanese trade. The tendency for a rapidly growing economy is to have declining relative prices in its export goods. This has happened in the case of the Japanese. They have been able to displace other higher-cost producers in market after market. The firms that are displaced naturally protest the market results.

Japan is an export powerhouse, but most of its production is for its own market. Japanese exports have grown more than twenty-one times in real terms from 1955 to 1985. However, Japanese real GNP has grown almost as fast. The growth in exports as a percentage of GNP has actually been lower for Japan than it has been for the United States, Germany, and other countries.

Japanese exports are now concentrated in machinery and transportation equipment (70%). Japan's changing comparative advantage over the postwar period has led to a decline in the share of basic manufactured goods in exports (presently 15%). In 1955, 58 percent of Japan's exports were basic manufactures and only 12 percent were machinery and transportation equipment. As Japan's technical and professional workforce and capital grew, Japan increased production of goods with a high engineering content, like automobiles and electronic equipment. It was able to establish leading positions in these differentiated products. Part of Japan's advantage was in having a flow of investment funds available for rapid movement into promising areas of global growth.

Japanese Imports

Japanese imports have also grown very rapidly over the postwar period. Imports in Japan increased in real terms more than twelve times from 1955 to 1985. Japan's share of global imports had risen to 6 percent in 1985, compared to 3 percent in 1955. This was in spite of a substantial Japanese trade surplus and a major U.S. trade deficit in 1985.

Japan's rapid growth has made it much more important to a number of countries as a market for their export goods. Japan takes 11 percent of the exports of the United States now, compared to 4 percent in 1955. Japan takes 47 percent of Indonesia's exports now, compared to 8 percent in 1955. Australia now sends more than 26 percent of its exports to Japan, compared to 8 percent in 1955.

The import pattern of Japan has changed considerably over the postwar period. Food and animal imports now account for less than half their value share in 1955. The share fell from 25 percent to 11 percent. Crude materials besides fuel account for less than a third of their value share in 1955. The share fell from 50 to 14 percent. The value share of fuels in imports has increased by more than three times over the postwar period. The share increased from 12 percent in 1955 to 43 percent in 1985. Taken together, these three categories of imports (foods, materials, and fuels) account for the lion's share of Japan's imports throughout the postwar period. They were 87 percent of the value of Japan's imports in 1955, and 68 percent in 1985.

There has been a modest increase in the share of Japanese imports in chemicals, basic manufactured goods, machinery and transportation equipment, and miscellaneous manufactures. As Japan's income continues to grow, it should increase imports in these areas of differentiated products. Japan's comparative disadvantage clearly is in the area of primary goods production. Its comparative advantage is in the area of manufacturing. It is unlikely that its import shares in manufacturing will dramatically change except with a major change in relative prices.

Barriers to International Trade

Japanese exporters have faced many barriers to their goods in overseas markets. In addition to tariffs and restrictions facing all imports, many countries have imposed special restrictions on imports from Japan. To some extent, this is a testimony to the successful development of the Japanese economy. The rapid growth, lower prices, and resulting displacement of other producers by Japan caused a political reaction in its trading partners. Nevertheless, it remains true that such barriers cause harm to consumers in the countries trading with Japan as well as hampering Japanese exporters. The United States and various countries in the EEC are the parties that have most often placed discriminatory barriers in the way of Japanese exports. These barriers are especially high on Japanese cars, steel, and consumer electronics.

The tariff barriers facing Japanese goods have been lowered over the postwar period through a series of multilateral negotiating sessions under the auspices of the General Agreement on Tariffs and Trade (GATT). Japan has been a full participant in these talks and has tended lately to make extra concessions in terms of accelerating the lowering of trade barriers. These concessions are usually responses to pressure put on Japan by its trading partners due to Japan's continued trade surplus. Since the initial effect of lower tariffs is to increase imports and thereby lower a trade surplus, Japan has accepted such changes. Nevertheless, Japan's trade surplus has remained high, because it is primarily caused by macroeconomic policies in the United States and Japan.

Japanese quantitative restrictions on trade have generally been lessened, and in many cases removed altogether. Japan still has substantial barriers to imports on agricultural goods, especially rice. The tariff equivalents of these agricultural barriers increased sharply with the appreciation of the yen in the 1980s. These barriers kept Japanese agricultural prices from falling along with other commodity prices. Japanese farmers escaped what would have been a sharp market adjustment. Instead, the farmers have benefited at the expense of Japanese consumers.

If all Japanese trade barriers were removed, there would be some increase in the relative income of farmers in the United States, Canada, and other countries with net agricultural exports. Japanese farmers would be reduced in number, and much of Japan's farmland would presumably be put to other uses. The consumers in Japan would see substantial gains in their welfare, as they no longer would have to pay seven times the world market price for rice or inflated prices for other agricultural goods.

Japan has much to gain from maintaining and increasing the free flow of goods and services in the global economy. Japan has concentrated its new productive capacity in areas of rapid global growth. It is dependent on global markets for imports of raw materials, food, and fuel. Japan's pattern of trade has reflected production according to comparative advantage more than many other industrial economies. Japan's factors of production are more different from the rest of the world's factors compared to the United States.

JAPAN'S MACROECONOMIC INTERACTIONS

Japan's economic changes have an increasingly large impact on the rest of the world. Japan now has more than four times the share of global GNP that it had in 1955. Japan's trading partners are thus much more interested in Japan's policies.

Japan has become the world's largest creditor nation and the United States the largest debtor nation, through the conjunction of the Reagan deficits and Japan's slower growth. Japan's economic growth is not as fast as it was in the period before the first oil shock. Japan's slower growth since 1974 has shaped the major effects it has had on the global economy. Japanese savings rates have declined less than domestic investment, which has contributed to an outflow of financial capital from Japan. Together with the increased demand for financial capital by the United States in the 1980s, this has caused unprecedented trade surpluses for Japan and trade deficits for the United States.

Japan's faster than average economic growth still tends to cause Japanese export prices to fall relative to other prices. This has the effect of causing distress in competitive industries in other countries. Consumer welfare increases all around the world because of the lower prices caused by Japan's growth. Some countries erect trade barriers to keep out Japanese goods.

Japan has become more of a global actor in financial markets. Part of Japan's liberalization of financial markets occurred due to a combination of domestic and international pressure for reform. Such changes have improved efficiency in an allocational sense. They also have contributed to a surge in Japanese holdings of foreign securities as Japanese financial institutions adjusted their portfolios.

Japan's decreased protectionism in virtually all categories except agriculture has had and will have only modest effects on Japan's trade surplus. When a trade barrier is lowered, the immediate effect is to raise imports and thereby lower a trade surplus. The general equilibrium effects are likely, over a period of time, to largely reverse this immediate effect. When foreigners export more to Japan, they will tend to spend more themselves, and this will tend to increase Japanese exports at least indirectly. When Japan imports more of the good with lower protection, imports of other goods will probably decline. These and other adjustments tend to reduce the impact of protection-easing measures on the trade balance. There are efficiency gains from such changes and they should be carried out, but macroeconomic changes are required to balance trade.

Japan is still extremely vulnerable to oil crises. The sharp oil price hikes in 1973–74 and 1979–80 had dramatic effects on Japan's economic performance. Since energy has been more than 40 percent of Japan's imports, whenever its relative price rises, Japan is heavily affected. Japan's real income falls. It has greater inflationary pressure, and the possibility of a recession. Lower energy prices helped Japan's real income growth during the latter part of the 1980s. If the price of oil goes higher and stays there, Japan will be harmed.

The Reagan deficits have led Japan to run greater trade surpluses than it otherwise would have. The United States has absorbed financial savings from around the world. Since Japan produces one of the largest pools of savings, it has been the source of much of the financial capital to support the U.S. budget deficit. Without sufficient offsetting financial flows in the other direction, the only way such financing can occur over a long period of time is for Japan to export more to the rest of the world than it imports. It has done so and has a large trade surplus. The United States has continued to run large trade deficits as it has failed to raise its national savings rate enough.

JAPAN AND GLOBAL INVESTMENT

The amount of net investment flows is largely a function of macroeconomic relationships. The composition and location of investment is determined by other economic variables. Pure diversification motives would result in substantial Japanese investment in capital markets abroad and substantial foreign investment in Japan.

The diversification motive appears to be strong for Japanese investors. Japanese foreign direct investment, which is easier to track by country and industry, is allocated among countries according to GNP. The higher a country's total GNP, the more Japanese foreign investment it is likely to receive. GNP is a rough measure of wealth, so this approximately corresponds to investing in a global market portfolio. Japanese foreign direct investment also responds positively to trade flows, especially to Japanese exports to a country. Japanese foreign direct investment has increased sharply in the service sector. It has sharply decreased in relative terms for mining. Japanese foreign direct investment in manufacturing has grown more slowly than investment in services, but much more rapidly than domestic Japanese investment.

Foreigners have invested over a trillion dollars in Japan. Most foreign investment is in short-term liquid assets. Only 27 percent of foreign investment is long term. Most of the long-term investment is portfolio investment in Japanese securities. Only a little more than 3 percent of foreign investment in Japan is in the form of foreign direct investment.

Foreign direct investment in Japan is more than 360 times its level in 1955. Still, it is only about 10 percent as large as Japanese foreign direct investment. Presently, it is difficult to tell whether foreign investment in Japan is so low because of continued barriers, even after liberalization, or if Japan is just not a good place in which to invest. Direct investment tends to occur when real assets are relatively cheap. With Japan's recent market value of the yen, Japanese assets are not cheap when viewed globally. Of course, the great fall in the Japanese stock market in 1990 has lowered the price of equity assets, but they are still high relative to expected earnings streams.

The United States has dominated direct foreign investment in Japan. It has held from 53 to 71 percent of foreign direct investment in Japan over the postwar period. Other countries with sizable foreign direct investments in Japan are the United Kingdom, West Germany, Switzerland, and Canada.

Foreign direct investment in Japan has been predominantly in manufacturing. The share of investment in manufacturing has declined, however, from over 90 percent in 1955 and 1965 to less than 70 percent in 1988. Foreign direct investment in commerce and real estate has grown rapidly in the 1980s, but it still represents a relatively small amount of total foreign direct investment in Japan.

JAPAN AND THE UNITED STATES

The United States has been the dominant global power in the postwar period. Even though Japan does not have total output that is equal to the United States, it has been gaining quickly on U.S. output levels. On a per capita basis, Japan has exceeded U.S. per capita income levels when income is compared using market exchange rates. Adjusted for differences in price levels, the United States still has a higher per capita income. Japan now has more than 85 percent of the U.S. per capita income level, even using purchasing power comparisons. This is amazing growth in Japan's relative income, since the Japanese per capita income was only 10 percent of the U.S. level in 1955.

Japanese wealth measured at market prices exceeded total wealth in the United States at the end of 1989, and probably still does. The only reason for doubt is the 40 percent fall in the Japanese stock market this year. The U.S. market had only fallen about 10 percent by the fall of 1990. Japanese real estate has up to four times the market value of U.S. real estate, even though there is much less of it.

Market wealth is so great in Japan, in part, because the Japanese have great confidence in their system. If the same discount rate were applied to the expected income stream of Japanese and U.S. assets, U.S. wealth would be greater. The greater confidence of the Japanese leads to a lower discount rate and a higher present value.

Japanese growth in income and real wealth is likely to continue at a faster pace than the rate in the United States. Japan is continuing to invest almost 50 percent more per dollar of GNP than is the United States. Japan's educational system performs extremely well at the primary and secondary levels. The United States provides a college level education for more of its citizens. A much higher percentage of women in the United States receive a college education. This is one of the few areas where the United States may have an advantage over the Japanese as regards economic efficiency.

Japan has more research and development professionals per worker than the United States. Japanese technology exports are growing faster than their technology imports, but they still import more technology than they export. They are also transferring a lot of technology through their direct foreign investment.

The United States and Japan are intense export competitors. Exchange rate policy is very important to the export industries in the two countries. In the early 1980s, the United States let the dollar become overvalued. Consequently, U.S. export industries were severely handicapped in holding market share around the world. It is in third markets, outside of the United States and Japan, that competition for market share is most intense. In these markets it is price and quality of goods that will determine market share. Protectionist policies at home will make it more difficult for export industries to perform in third markets. Of the four top exports of Japan, three are also top exports of the United States.

The United States and Japan do not have the same kind of import pattern. The only top import they have in common is oil. The United States is the largest provider of Japanese imports. Japan is the top provider of U.S. imports. West Germany is the only country that has been among the top four exporting countries to both the United States and Japan. Part of the reason is proximity. Canada and Mexico are major exporters to the United States; Indonesia is among the top exporters to Japan. Saudi Arabia is also among the top four exporters to Japan.

The United States and Japan both have substantial trade barriers. The United States has restrictive nontariff barriers on textiles, steel, and automobiles. Japan has nontariff barriers primarily on agricultural goods and textiles. These nontariff barriers change in their tariff equivalents year by year. They are not as predictable and are more perverse in their market distortions than tariffs would be.

Japan has been much more successful than the United States in achieving macroeconomic goals in the 1980s. Japan has had real economic growth of 3.2 percent per capita per year in the 1980s, which is about double the rate for the United States. Japan has had an average unemployment rate of 2.5 percent in the 1980s, compared to 7.6 percent in the United States. This indicates that the United States foregoes much more potential output because of macroeconomic imbalances. At the same time, Japan has held inflation to 2.7 percent over the 1980s, compared to the U.S. level of 5.8 percent. By maintaining the macroeconomy in a balanced and predictable state, Japanese policymakers provide a better economic environment for management and labor. Better private market decisions tend to result from the more stable environment.

JAPAN AND LESS DEVELOPED COUNTRIES

Dynamic global efficiency requires exchanges over time at optimal levels as well as exchanges between nations. One of the most important sets of exchanges is that between capital-rich countries like Japan and the less developed countries. LDCs have a need for more education and physical capital. If Japan provides some of those resources now, it can enjoy higher consumption later, when the LDCs repay the capital transfer. A critical linkage is the eventual repayment of resources provided. Japan has a major stake in developing necessary multilateral mechanisms for efficient intertemporal transfer of resources.

Japan is now the leading donor nation to LDCs. This role may shift back and forth between the United States and Japan, depending upon current exchange rates. Nevertheless, Japan has clearly reached the top level of nations in the overall voluntary giving of aid to LDCs.

Japan's trade with and investment in LDCs is even more important to LDC growth than Japanese aid. Japan tends to run a trade deficit (or less of a surplus) with LDCs, and a trade surplus with developed countries like the United States and members of the EEC. This facilitates the growth of LDCs by providing them with markets for their products. Japan's openness to these countries' exports will be critical as their development accelerates. Japan's direct investment in LDCs helps promote their growth by providing capital and technology for modern manufacturing.

SUMMARY

Japan's rapid economic growth shapes every connection of Japan with the rest of the world. Japan's import and export patterns have changed significantly over the last forty years, and its comparative advantage changed as Japanese capital accumulation occurred. The rapid growth of

Japanese exports has caused many countries to erect discriminatory barriers to Japan's exports. Japan has been able to position itself favorably in expanding global markets because of its rapid capital accumulation.

Rapid growth has assisted Japan in maintaining low unemployment. Low unemployment in turn helps economic growth, by allowing more consumption and investment. In spite of rapid growth, Japan has avoided, for the most part, inflationary excesses. When growth in Japan slowed to levels that were still much higher than in the United States, it left high savings levels available for use in foreign markets.

The Reagan deficits and excess savings in Japan combined to bring about large trade imbalances. Fiscal excess in the United States, together with a strong dollar, led to large trade deficits with the rest of the world. Most of the excess savings were provided by Japan and West Germany. The United States has yet to raise its national savings rate sufficiently to balance its trade. Even with global trade balanced, the United States would probably run a deficit with Japan.

Japan's rapid growth is an inspiration to policymakers in LDCs around the world. They could hardly hope to do better than to replicate the Japanese "miracle" of rapid sustained growth with macroeconomic stability. A key element in Japan's growth has been its production for global markets using resources obtained from global markets. The benefits of international trade can clearly be seen in the example of Japan. If Japan can further assist in the development of others in a global trading economy, the whole world will benefit.

BIBLIOGRAPHY

American Chamber of Commerce Researchers Association. *Cost of Living Index.* Louisville, Ky.: ACCRA, various issues.

Balassa, Bela, and Marcus Noland. *Japan in the World Economy.* Washington, D.C.: Institute for International Economics, 1988.

Baldwin, Nick, and Richard Prosser. "World Oil Market Simulation." *Energy Economics* 10(July 1988):185–98.

Baldwin, Robert E. "The Changing Nature of U.S. Trade Policy since World War II." In *The Structure and Evolution of Recent U.S. Trade Policy,* edited by Robert E. Baldwin and Anne O. Krueger. Chicago: University of Chicago Press, 1984.

______. "The Political Economy of Postwar U.S. Trade Policy." In *International Trade and Finance: Readings,* 2d ed., edited by Robert E. Baldwin and J. David Richardson. Boston: Little, Brown, 1981.

Baldwin, Robert E., and Anne O. Krueger, eds. *The Structure and Evolution of Recent U.S. Trade Policy.* Chicago: University of Chicago Press, 1984.

Baldwin, Robert E., and J. David Richardson, eds. *International Trade and Finance: Readings.* 2d ed. Boston: Little, Brown, 1981.

Bergsten, C. Fred, and William R. Cline. *The United States-Japan Economic Problem.* Washington, D.C.: Institute for International Economics, 1987.

Berthet-Bondet, Claude, Derek Blades, and Annie Pin. "The OECD Compatible Trade and Production Data Base, 1970–1985." OECD Department of Economics and Statistics, *Working Papers,* no. 60, November 1988.

Bhagwati, Jagdish N., ed. *The Brain Drain and Taxation: Theory and Empirical Analysis.* Amsterdam: North Holland, 1976.

Boskin, Michael J. "Taxation, Saving, and the Rate of Interest." *Journal of Political Economy.* 86 (April 1978):S3–27.

Brodin, Anders, and Derek Blades. "The OECD Compatible Trade and Production Data Base, 1970–1983." OECD Department of Economics and Statistics, *Working Papers,* no. 31, March 1986.

Buchanan, James M., and Gordon Tullock. *The Calculus of Consent: Logical Foundations of Constitutional Democracy.* Ann Arbor: University of Michigan Press, Ann Arbor Paperbacks, 1967.

Caves, Richard E., Jeffrey A. Frankel, and Ronald W. Jones. *World Trade and Payments: An Introduction.* Glenview, Ill.: Scott Foresman/Little, Brown Higher Education, 1990.

Chandler, Clay, and Marcus W. Brauchli. "Oil Security, How Japan Became So Energy Efficient: It Leaned on Industry." *The Wall Street Journal,* September 10, 1990, A1.

Chen, Nai-fu, Richard Roll, and Stephen A. Ross. "Economic Forces and the Stock Market." *Journal of Business* 59 (July 1986): 383–403.

Cho, D. C., C. Eun, and L. W. Senbet. "International Arbitrage Pricing Theory: An Empirical Investigation." *Journal of Finance* 41 (June 1986): 313–29.

Curtis, Thomas B., and John Robert Vastine, Jr. *The Kennedy Round and the Future of American Trade.* New York: Praeger, 1971.

Deardorff, Alan V. "The General Validity of the Heckscher-Ohlin Theorem." *American Economic Review* 72 (September 1982):683-94.

Deardorff, Alan V., and Robert M. Stern. "A Computational Analysis of Alternative Scenarios for Multilateral Trade Liberalization," in process, 1987. Cited in Gary R. Saxonhouse and Robert M. Stern. "An Analytical Survey of Formal and Informal Barriers to International Trade and Investment in the United States, Canada, and Japan." In *Trade and Investment Relations Among the United States, Canada and Japan,* edited by Robert M. Stern. Chicago: University of Chicago Press, 1989.

______. "The Effects of the Tokyo Round on the Structure of Protection." In *The Structure and Evolution of Recent U.S. Trade Policy,* edited by Robert E. Baldwin and Anne O. Krueger. Chicago: University of Chicago Press, 1984.

______. *The Michigan Model of World Production and Trade: Theory and Applications.* Cambridge, Mass.: MIT Press, 1986.

Denison, Edward Fulton. *Why Growth Rates Differ: Postwar Experience in Nine Western Countries.* Washington, D.C.: The Brookings Institution, 1967.

Dixit, Avinash, and Victor Norman. *Theory of International Trade.* Cambridge, England: Cambridge University Press, 1980.

Energy Information Administration, U.S. Department of Energy. *Annual Energy Review, 1989.* Washington, D.C., May 24, 1990.

Feldman, Robert Alan. *Japanese Financial Markets: Deficits, Dilemmas, and Deregulation.* Cambridge, Mass.: MIT Press, 1986.

Feldstein, M., and C. Horioka. "Domestic Saving and International Capital Flows." *Economic Journal* 90 (1980):314–29.

Gibson, Roger C. *Asset Allocation: Balancing Financial Risk,* Homewood, Ill.: Dow Jones-Irwin, 1990.

Grubel, Herbert G., and P. J. Lloyd. *Intra-Industry Trade: The Theory and Measurement of International Trade in Differentiated Products.* New York: Wiley, 1975.

Guilford, J. P., and Benjamin Fruchter. *Fundamental Statistics in Psychology and Education.* 5th ed. New York: McGraw-Hill, 1973.

Harrington, Diana R., Frank J. Fabozzi, and H. Russell Fogler. *The New Stock Market.* Chicago: Probus, 1990.

Hayami, Y., and M. Honma. *Reconsideration of Agricultural Policy.* Tokyo: The Forum for Policy Innovation, February 1987.

Hayashi, Fumio. "Is Japan's Saving Rate High?" *Quarterly Review of the Federal Reserve Bank of Minneapolis* (Spring 1989):3–9.

Helpman, Elhanan, and Paul R. Krugman. *Market Structure and Foreign Trade: Increasing Returns, Imperfect Competition, and the International Economy.* Cambridge, Mass.: MIT Press, 1985.

Higashi, Chikara, and Peter G. Lauter. *The Internationalization of the Japanese Economy.* Boston: Kluwer, 1987.

Ho, Alfred K. *Japan's Trade Liberalization in the 1960s.* New York: International Arts and Sciences Press, 1973.

Honeygold, Derek. *International Financial Markets.* New York: Nichols, 1989.

Honma, Masayoshi. "Comment" on paper by Andrew Schmitz. In *Trade and Investment Relations among the United States, Canada and Japan,* edited by Robert M. Stern. Chicago: University of Chicago Press, 1989.

Honma, M., and Y. Hayami. "Structure of Agriculture Protection in Industrial Countries." *Journal of International Economics,* 20 (February 1986): 115–29.

Houthakker, H. S., and Stephen P. Magee. "Income and Price Elasticities in World Trade." *Review of Economics and Statistics* 51 (May 1969): 111–25.

International Labour Office. *Yearbook of Labour Statistics.* Geneva: International Labour Organization, various years.

International Monetary Fund. *Annual Report on Exchange Restrictions.* Washington, D.C., 1956.

International Monetary Fund. *International Financial Statistics.* Washington, D.C.: IMF, various issues.

Japan Economic Institute. *Japan's Foreign Direct Investment in Developing Countries.* JEI Report no. 31A, August 11, 1989.

______. *Statistical Profile: Japan's Economy in 1988 and International Transactions of Japan and the United States in 1988.* JEI Report no. 39A, October 13, 1989.

______. *Japan's Foreign Aid Policy.* JEI Report no. 41A, October 27, 1989.

______. *Japan as an International Creditor: New Economic and Political Realities.* JEI Report no. 42A, November 3, 1989.

Japan Institute for Social and Economic Affairs. *Japan 1986: An International Comparison,* Tokyo: Keizai Koho Center Cited in Chikara Higashi and Peter G. Lauter. *The Internationalization of the Japanese Economy.* Boston: Kluwer, 1987.

______. *Japan 1989: An International Comparison.* Tokyo: Keizai Koho Center, 1988.

Jorgenson, Dale W. "Productivity and Economic Growth in Japan and the United States." *American Economic Review Proceedings* 78 (May 1988): 217–28.

Kindleberger, Charles P. *The World in Depression, 1929–1939.* 2d ed. Berkeley: University of California Press, 1986.

Klein, Roger W. "A Dynamic Theory of Comparative Advantage." *American Economic Review* 63 (March 1973): 173–84.

Kravis, Irving B., et al. *A System of International Comparisons of Gross Product and Purchasing Power.* Baltimore: Johns Hopkins University Press (for the World Bank), 1975.

Krugman, Paul R. *Exchange Rate Instability.* The Lionel Robbins Lectures (1989), Cambridge, Mass.: MIT Press, 1989.

Lavergne, Real Phillipe. "The Political Economy of U.S. Tariffs." Ph.D. diss., University of Toronto, 1981.

Leamer, Edward E. *Sources of International Comparative Advantage: Theory and Evidence.* Cambridge, Mass.: MIT Press, 1984.

Lincoln, Edward J. *Japan: Facing Economic Maturity.* Washington, D.C.: The Brookings Institution, 1988.

Lipsey, Richard G., and Peter O. Steiner. *Economics.* 6th ed. New York: Harper & Row, 1981.

McKinnon, Ronald I. "Protectionism and the Misaligned Dollar: The Case for Monetary Coordination." In *The New Protectionist Threat to World Welfare,* edited by Dominick Salvatore. Amsterdam: North Holland, 1987.

Meynell, Benedict. "Relations with Japan: The Problem and the European Community's Response." In *Japan and Western Europe,* edited by Loukas Tsoukalis and Maureen White. New York: St. Martin's Press, 1982.

Moffat, Susan. "Meet Your New Japanese Landlord." *Fortune,* June 18, 1990.

Monk-Turner, Elizabeth A., and Yoko Baba. "Gender and College Opportunities: Changes over Time in the United States and Japan." *Sociological Inquiry* 57 (Summer 1987):292–303.

Morgan Guaranty Trust Company. *World Financial Markets.* November 22, 1989.

National Center for Education Statistics. *Digest of Education Statistics, 1989.* Washington, D.C.: Government Printing Office, 1989.

Neumann, George R. "Adjustment Assistance for Trade-Displaced Workers." In *International Trade and Finance: Readings,* 2d ed., edited by Robert E. Baldwin and J. David Richardson. Boston: Little, Brown, 1981.

Office of the Prime Minister, Bureau of Statistics. *Japan Statistical Yearbook.* Tokyo: various years.

Oniki, H., and Hirofumi Uzawa. "Patterns of Trade and Investment in a Dynamic Model of International Trade." *Review of Economic Studies* 32 (January 1965):15–38.

Organization for Economic Cooperation and Development. *OECD Economic Outlook: Historical Statistics, 1960–1987.* Paris: OECD, 1989.

Porter, Michael E., ed. *Competition in Global Industries.* Boston: Harvard Business School Press, 1986.

Poterba, James M., and Lawrence H. Summers. "Mean Reversion in Stock Prices: Evidence and Implications." *Journal of Financial Economics* 22 (October 1988):27–59.

Qureshi, Usman A., Raymond Strangways, and Charlie G. Turner. "Human Skill

Intensity in International Trade." Paper presented at Southwestern Society of Economists, Houston, Tx., 1986.

Rawls, John. *A Theory of Justice.* Cambridge, Mass.: Harvard University Press, 1971.

Ricardo, David. *On the Principles of Political Economy and Taxation.* London: John Murray, 1817.

Roningen, Vernon, and Alexander Yeats. "Nontariff Distortions of International Trade: Some Preliminary Empirical Evidence." *Weltwirtschaftliches Archiv* 112 (1976):613–25.

Ross, Stephen. "The Arbitrage Theory of Capital Asset Pricing." *Journal of Economic Theory* 13 (December 1976):341–60.

Salvatore, Dominick, ed. *The New Protectionist Threat to World Welfare.* Amsterdam: North Holland, 1987.

Saxonhouse, Gary R., and Robert M. Stern. "An Analytical Survey of Formal and Informal Barriers to International Trade and Investment in the United States, Canada, and Japan." In *Trade and Investment Relations Among the United States, Canada, and Japan,* edited by Robert M. Stern. Chicago: University of Chicago Press, 1989.

Sazanami, Yoko. "Trade and Investment Patterns in the United States, Canada and Japan." In *Trade and Investment Relations among the United States, Canada and Japan,* edited by Robert M. Stern. Chicago: University of Chicago Press, 1989.

Sekiguchi, Sueo. *Japanese Direct Foreign Investment: An Atlantic Institute Research Volume.* Montclair: Allanheld, Osmun, 1979.

______. "Japanese Direct Investment in Europe." In *Japan and Western Europe,* edited by Loukas Tsoukalis and Maureen White. New York: St. Martin's Press, 1982.

Shepherd, Geoffrey. "Japanese Exports and Europe's Problem Industries." In *Japan and Western Europe,* edited by Loukas Tsoukalis and Maureen White. New York: St. Martin's Press, 1982.

Shiller, Robert J. "Theories of Aggregate Stock Price Movements." *Journal of Portfolio Management* (Winter 1984):28–37.

Solnick, Bruno. *International Investments.* Reading, Mass.: Addison-Wesley, 1988.

Solow, Robert M. *Growth Theory: An Exposition.* Oxford: Clarendon, 1970.

Spence, A. Michael. Class lectures on Oligopoly in Microeconomics. Harvard University, 1976.

Staiger, Robert W., Alan V. Deardorff, and Robert M. Stern. "Employment Effects of Japanese and American Protectionism." In *The New Protectionist Threat to World Welfare,* edited by Dominick Salvatore. Amsterdam: North Holland, 1987.

Stern, Robert M., ed. *Trade and Investment Relations among the United States, Canada and Japan.* Chicago: University of Chicago Press, 1989.

Stolper, Wolfgang F., and Paul A. Samuelson. "Protection and Real Wages." *Review of Economic Studies* 9 (1941):58–73.

Summers, Lawrence, and Chris Carroll. "Why is U.S. National Saving So Low?" *Brookings Papers on Economic Activity,* no. 2 (1987):607–35.

Suzuki, Yoshio. *Money, Finance, and Macroeconomic Performance in Japan*. New Haven: Yale University Press, 1986.

Tarr, David G., and Morris E. Morkre. "Aggregate Costs to the United States of Tariffs and Quotas on Imports." In *The New Protectionist Threat to World Welfare,* edited by Dominick Salvatore. Amsterdam: North Holland, 1987.

Tsoukalis, Loukas, and Maureen White, eds. *Japan and Western Europe.* New York: St. Martin's Press, 1982.

Turner, Charlie G. "Japanese Import Restrictions." *Quarterly Review of Economics and Business* 29 (Spring 1989):82–91.

———. *Quantitative Restrictions on International Trade of the United States and Japan.* Ph.D. diss., Harvard University, 1981.

———. "Stock Market Returns, Keynes' Investor Confidence, and Gamma, a Measure of Dynamic Efficiency." Paper presented at the Economics Seminar, Old Dominion University, September, 1990.

———. "Two Simple Measures of Dynamic Efficiency in the Global Economy." *Quarterly Review of Economics and Business* 27 (Autumn 1987):40–55.

———. "Voluntary Export Restraints on Trade Going to the United States." *Southern Economic Journal,* 49 (January 1983):793–803.

United Nations. Department of International Economic and Social Affairs. *World Population Prospects,* 1988. Population Studies, no. 106. New York: United Nations, 1989.

United Nations. Statistical Office. *Yearbook of International Trade Statistics.* New York: United Nations, various years.

United Nations. Statistical Office. *Yearbook of National Accounts Statistics.* New York: United Nations, various years.

United States Bureau of the Census. *County and City Data Book.* Washington, D.C.: Government Printing Office, various years.

United States Department of Agriculture. *Agricultural Statistics.* Washington, D.C.: Government Printing Office, various years.

United States Department of Commerce. Bureau of Economic Analysis. *Business Conditions Digest.* Washington, D.C.: Government Printing Office, various issues.

United States President. *Economic Report of the President.* Washington, D.C.: Government Printing Office, various years.

INDEX

About the Author

CHARLIE G. TURNER is Associate Professor of Economics at Old Dominion University. He teaches international economics and international finance at the graduate and undergraduate levels. His current research interests are in the areas of dynamic efficiency, international capital markets, Japan, and trade barriers. He has published articles in the *Quarterly Review of Economics and Business*, the *Journal of Economic History*, and *Studies in Economic Analysis*.